George W Strettell

A new Source of Revenue for India

George W Strettell

A new Source of Revenue for India

ISBN/EAN: 9783337058883

Printed in Europe, USA, Canada, Australia, Japan

Cover: Foto ©ninafisch / pixelio.de

More available books at **www.hansebooks.com**

A

NEW SOURCE OF REVENUE

FOR

INDIA.

BY

GEORGE W. STRETTELL,

H.M.'s Indian Forest Department.

"*Magna est veritas et prævalebit.*"

LONDON: MARLBOROUGH & CO., 51, OLD BAILEY.

BRIGHTON: JOHN BEAL & CO., 55, EAST STREET.

1878.

Price Two Shillings.

PREFACE.

In putting forth this little pamphlet, I beg leave to state very briefly the objects with which it has been written, and the considerations which have induced me to publish it.

It has often struck me, while engaged in my official duties in the Indian Forest Department, that a large revenue might be derived from plants which are looked upon as mere weeds—plants which require no care in cultivation; which will grow in land utterly unsuited to any other crops; which yield fibre which has been practically proved to be well adapted to the manufacture of paper, and textile fabrics.

At a time when famine has once more seriously embarrassed the finances of the Indian Empire, it seems to me that I should be failing in my duty, if I did not draw prominent attention to a source of revenue which has, for reasons which I have attempted to give, hitherto remained comparatively neglected.

I have, in the following pages, advocated the cultivation —at first, if need be, experimentally, and on a small scale —of several different plants, and especially of one, the *Calotropis gigantea.** The fibre of this plant has been pronounced by paper-makers, and manufacturers of textile fabrics, as excellent; and I have shown, I hope, convincingly,

* As this plant is mentioned in works dating as far back as 1839, it may be imagined that there is some occult reason why it should not have been used. The fact is that the idea of utilizing it was abandoned on the strength of certain imperfect and inconclusive experiments, which tended to shew that the cost of preparing the fibre was greater than its market value. As I have said in the following pages, the substitution of machinery for manual labour would greatly reduce the cost of the preparation of the fibre. This has not yet been attempted.

that, after allowing for the cost of cultivation and of extracting the fibre, the raw material might be sold at such a price as to add considerably to the Imperial revenue.

I have given my reasons for thinking that the development of the fibre trade of India should, at all events, in the first instance, be undertaken by the Government, and not left to the enterprise of merchants; and I am glad to know that her Majesty's Secretary of State for India is of the same opinion. We have to deal in the East with a people entirely different from our own countrymen; and I would earnestly beg the English reader, who has not lived in the East, to consider the arguments I have brought forward in support of my position, before he forms an opinion on this matter.*

The great practical interest which the Indian Government has taken in the preparation of rheea fibre, and the readiness which it has always shewn to encourage the development of the resources of the country, are sufficient guarantee that it will not allow a matter of such importance to remain unexamined; and I am confident that experiment will shew my hopes to be well grounded.

The matter is one of exceptional interest, at a time when the supply of the principal material hitherto in use for paper-making is insufficient for the demand; and when considerable anxiety prevails regarding the jute† trade, which is apparently in a languishing condition.

I have devoted much time and thought to the subject of this pamphlet, and should be very grateful for any suggestions that may occur to the reader. I am convinced that, sooner or later, the matter will be taken up by English merchants in India, and I am altogether of opinion that it should ultimately be left in their hands. But it

* *Vide* paragraph 33, Part I.

† I would invite the reader's special attention to the portion of this pamphlet (pp. 69—75) in which I have contrasted jute and the *Calotropis gigantea* as fibre-yielding plants, &c.

seems to me, for the reasons which the reader will find stated at the pages already referred to, that the authorities in England and India should take the first step to establish the industry; and I should have thought myself wanting in loyal duty to the Government whose servant I have the honour to be, had I not placed before it the advantages which would accrue from the encouragement of the cultivation of the plants in question. I conceive it to be the duty of every loyal servant of the Government to act up to the spirit of the instructions issued by the Governor-General of India, in Council, to Dr. Buchanan Hamilton, seventy years ago, when the first attempt was made to carry out a statistical survey of Bengal. "Should it appear," says his Excellency, "that any new object of cultivation could be introduced with advantage, you will suggest the means by which its introduction may be encouraged."

In obedience to this command, which I consider to be still morally incumbent on every Indian official, I have written the following pages. If I succeed in inducing the Government to take action in the matter, with a view of testing the accuracy or otherwise of my anticipations, I shall be amply rewarded.

I cannot conclude these prefatory remarks without expressing my sincere acknowledgments to Colonel Sir W. MEREWETHER, K.C.S.I., C.B., for the very courteous manner in which he has supplied me with valuable information on the subject of this pamphlet.

PART I.

For years past it has been my delight to collect Introductory. the natural products of our tropical forests, in the hope of one day ascertaining their commercial value. Hitherto, owing to circumstances over which I have had no control, my hopes have not been realized. At last, however, an opportunity, of which I gladly avail myself, occurs of turning to advantage the experience I have gained in the Forest Department of India during the last nineteen years.

1. The value of Bamboo as a paper-producing Bamboo as a paper-making material. material has recently been shown by Mr. Thomas Routledge,* who has spared himself no trouble in detailing what appears to him the most economical process of turning this valuable product to account.

2. In consequence, to some extent, of the appear- Early Government experiments with bamboo. ance of his pamphlet, the authorities in British Burma resolved to make experiments, and I was deputed by the Conservator of Forests to plant one acre of ground with each of the four commonest varieties of Bamboo, with a view to ascertaining their relative fibre-yielding capabilities.

---

*Bamboo considered as a Paper-making Material. By T. Routledge. E. and F. N. Spon, London, 1875.

I did so, but was prevented from further watching the development of the project by my departure for England on two years' furlough. The scheme has since, I believe, attained larger proportions, but, if I am rightly informed, it still remains uncertain whether the undertaking will prove a financial success.

3. The manufacture of paper from Bamboo is no new discovery, it has been practised by the Chinese for centuries past; and more recently our trans-Atlantic neighbours have turned the plant to the same account. It only remains, then, for me to consider the political and financial merits of the scheme so far as India is concerned.

Paper made from bamboo by the Chinese.

4. Before proceeding to do so, however, I should mention as a proof of the deep practical interest I take in the opening up of the fibre trade of India, that I have submitted for the approval of the Government of British Burma five samples of paper made from the fibres of (1) *Ficus Rumphii,* (2) *Ficus infectoria,* (3) *Ficus affinis,* (4) *Streblus aspera, and* (5) *Broussonetia papyrifera.*

Samples of paper submitted by the author to Government.

5. These fibres, and specially the two last named, appear to me to be at least as well suited as bamboo for the requirements of the paper-trade, and the strongest argument against the utilization of bamboo for the manufacture of paper does not hold in the case of the plants which I have named. Bamboo is a necessary of every-day life to the poorest natives of India. Of it they make their simple huts, and it is the material of which their rude

Arguments against utilization of bamboo for paper-making.

furniture is generally formed. If it once became an article of export, its price would rise so rapidly, that it would soon be beyond the reach of the natives who are so dependent on it. Whether any increase of revenue, however great, would not be too dearly bought at such a price is a question for very serious consideration; and the reason which determined the Government to exempt bamboo from taxation (in Burma) will no doubt carry equal weight when they come to consider the question of its export for the purpose of paper manufacture. The Government felt that to levy a tax on this product would be to deprive the hill tribes of their chief means of gaining a livelihood, and feared that such a deprivation might act as an incentive to crime. In like manner, when it was contemplated to check the destructive habit of *toungya** cultivation, it was urged that the tribes, who are dependent on this rude mode of culture, are a barbarous race, who, though rude and ignorant, are not destitute of spirit; and that to attempt summarily to deprive them of their only means of livelihood would be simply to drive them to cattle-lifting and other crime, if not to open rebellion; while if they fled the country, the last state of the forests would be worse than the first. The same argument applies with not less force to the question of the utilization of Bamboo for paper-making. The gradual development of revenue, when regulated with due regard to the condition of the people, is an undeniable blessing, but more harm than good results

*A system of cultivation practised by the hill tribes, who burn large forest areas, and subsequently cultivate the sites so cleared.

from too precipitate measures ; the people are forced to live beyond their means, and are thus induced to seek a dishonest livelihood ; in short, an impetus is given to crime, in order that the revenue may benefit. This, it need hardly be said, is in direct opposition to every principle of political economy.

My object in writing this essay is to shew that the revenue of India may be largely increased, the requirements of the paper-trade being at the same time duly considered, without incurring the dangers to which I have referred.

6. Before stating my own views however, I propose to consider those contained in Mr. Routledge's pamphlet on Bamboo, not with the object of detracting from his proposition, but rather to caution Government against engaging in an enterprise which may ultimately prove a financial failure, as well as a political error. The ill-success which has attended many of our experiments, is in a great measure, I fear, to be attributed to a disregard of the old maxim " Look before you leap "; and there is no doubt that the more important the project, the greater is the necessity for careful deliberation before embarking on it.

7. Mr. Routledge starts by telling us that, " *Of all the fibre-yielding plants known to botanical science there is not one so well calculated to meet the pressing requirements of the paper-trade as Bamboo, both as regards facility and economy of production, as well as the quality of the paper-stock which can be manufactured therefrom : grown under*

11

favourable conditions of climate and soil, there is no plant which will give so heavy a crop of available fibre to the acre, no plant which requires so little care for its cultivation and continuous production."

This statement the author supports by referring to the rapidity of growth of the bamboo, and its wide geographical distribution; and he then proceeds to figures.

8. To prevent any misunderstanding, and to *Mr. Routledge's scheme examined.* shew what appears to me the weakest point in Mr. Routledge's scheme, it is only due to him that I should reproduce his estimates before proceeding to analyze them. The authorities will thus be able to contrast the respective merits of our propositions with the least possible trouble.

9. At page 8, Mr. Routledge writes :—" *Allowing* *Mr. Routledge's esti- mate of out-turn.* 208 *feet square to represent one acre; divided into twelve beds, each* 96 × 26 *feet with twelve paths* 96' × 8' 8 *wide, and one intersecting road* 208 × 16 *feet wide, leaves a space for planting equal to* 2496 *feet, or* 29,952 *feet in the twelve beds; allowing the stems to be* 2 *feet apart, and say only* 12 *feet high, we have* 7488 *stems, which at* 12 *lbs. each equal* 40 *tons per acre.*"

10. Anyone who has had practical experience in *The habits of the bamboo.* bamboo culture, and is familiar with the habits of the plant in its natural home, must feel that the surest and cheapest method of reproducing it is by division of its roots,—a system that not only recommends itself on grounds of economy, but on the score of preservation of species, with the smallest

percentage of failure. It must be understood that the numerous varieties of bamboo which are to be found in British Burma do not in every instance grow in distinct or separate areas, though it is perhaps the exception to find more than two varieties intermixed. Mr. Kurz, in his valuable work on the Forests of Pegu,* has divided jungle-fires into two classes,—superficial † and destructive : the latter he tells us "do not occur annually, but periodically, and set in after the bamboo has come into flower." Elsewhere he says, that " all the bamboo stocks usually flower together at the same time, and this is the case also with those growing as undergrowth in the forest ; they then die off, one by one, after maturing their seed. It is believed," he adds, " that they do so regularly after a certain number of years, which is variously set down at from 40 to 60 years. For the larger kinds this may be a fair estimate ; but I know of a bamboo in Java, 25 feet high, which flowers, and dies off every three years, and of others which flower regularly at the ends of the branches for many years (especially Schizostachya), until they finally become a whole gigantic panicule of flowers ere the close of their lives."

11. The inference to be drawn from this extract

Bamboo best propagated by division of roots. is, that bamboo plantations must be carefully protected from fire, and that seed is not at all times obtainable. This latter

* Preliminary Report on the Forests of Pegu. By Sulpice Kurz . C. B. Lewis, Calcutta.

† The superficial fires the author tells us occur " *annually*," and are " *really fearful.*"

difficulty might perhaps in a measure be overcome, were it not that when seed is kept in store it is rapidly destroyed by insects. Moreover, even if a sufficient supply of seed is available at the required time, it is almost impossible to be sure that different varieties have not been mixed ; for the natives, on whom we must entirely depend for the collections of the seeds, are not sufficiently scrupulous and careful to guarantee a preservation of species. For these reasons it will not always be convenient or profitable to cultivate bamboo from seed, and I have therefore proposed—when practicable—to propagate the plant by division of its roots.

12. Assuming then that we have to plant one acre Mr. Routledge's estimate examined. subdivided in the manner suggested by Mr. Routledge, the actual area left available for planting is 29,652 square feet. This stocked at intervals of 6′ x 6′ gives about 831 plants. Now the habit of the bamboo forbids an absolute annual clearance, and the maximum number of succulent shoots that each clump ought to be deprived of should not, according to my experience, exceed five. We have thus an annual yield of 4,155 green stems, or about 22¼ tons (allowing that each stem weighs 12lbs.) or a little over 5½ tons of dried stems, allowing 75 per cent. for dissipation of moisture. This reduces Mr. Routledge's estimate nearly 50 per cent. ; and the cost of producing this quantity would, at the current rate of labour in Burma, be Rs. 26, or £2 7s. 8d. taking the rupee at 1s. 10d.

13. On the same page (8), Mr. Routledge

14

Mr. Routledge's scheme not economical. proposes to increase the yield per acre, by making several annual cuttings. Knowing that the bamboo only sends out one set of shoots in the year, I wrote and asked the author to kindly elucidate his meaning ; and he tells me that he proposes to stimulate growth by a system of artificial irrigation ; in fact, to use nearly his own words, he would pursue a system almost analogous to that followed in the culture of asparagus, and with meadows under sewage or plain irrigation. The heavy cost which such a process would necessarily involve, of itself, to my mind, condemns his proposition on the ground of economy alone.

14. I will now go on to consider the operations Further details of Mr. Routledge's proposal. following the delivery of the green stems at the central factory. Mr. Routledge writes at page 11 :—" Now although the stems of Bamboo, after cutting and crushing, may, as I have shewn, be dried (and will when dried give a yield of 60 per cent. of fibre), still their bulk and extreme lightness would preclude importing them to this country, not merely from their heavy cost of carriage, but from their liability to damage from fermentation. For these economical considerations, therefore, I propose to reduce the Bamboo into fibrous stock where grown or produced." At p. 10 the author explains the process requisite to reduce the dried, succulent stems to fibrous stock in the following words : " The stems are passed through heavy crushing rolls in order to split and flatten them, and at the same time crushing the knots or

15

nodes. The stems thus flattened are passed through a second series of rolls, which are channelled or grooved, in order further to split, or partially divide, them longitudinally into strips or ribbons; these being cut transversely into convenient lengths, by a guillotine knife or shears, are delivered by a carrier or automatic feeder direct to the boiling pans or elsewhere as desired." Then at page 14, he goes on to say : " I have now only further to remark that the plant required to manufacture paper-stock from bamboo on an economical and practical working scale would consist of a battery of boiling pans, with the other necessary adjuncts and machinery, steam-engines and steam-boilers, such plant being on a scale adequate to the manufacture of 100 tons Bamboo weekly, producing therefrom say 60 tons of merchantable paper-stock."

15. For ready reference, I will now contrast in a condensed form Mr. Routledge's estimate of cost for carrying out his system, with my computation of the probable expenditure that would have to be incurred. Mr. Routledge gives £10 as the cost of cultivating one acre of bamboo, which is to yield 40 tons of green stems delivered at the central factory at the rate of 5s. per ton ; these 40 tons to yield six tons of paper-stock.

16. Now, according to my estimate, in which I have not included land rent, artificial irrigation, cutting, delivery at the central factory, charge for supervision, value of machinery and its indispensable adjuncts, but which only

allows for cost of survey, clearing of land, pitting, making of roads, value of roots, cost of transplanting, and sundries (including wear and tear of tools), one acre will only yield 22½ tons of green stems, or 5½ of dried stems, at a cost of £2 7s. 8d. It seems to me, therefore, that adding the charges which I have not included in my calculation, the aggregate cost would be so great as to forbid a continuance of the undertaking.

17. I may of course be wrong and Mr. Routledge *Which estimate is correct?* right; but our respective estimates vary to such a striking extent that a searching investigation seems desirable with a view to arriving at a just conclusion as to their comparative merits. Having the interest of India at heart, I shall be agreeably surprised if, after careful inquiry, Mr. Routledge's proposition proves to be practicable ; indeed I shall hail with delight the advent of bamboo into the European market, for the vastness of the paper-trade affords ample room for the introduction of bamboo, as well as of the different fibres to which I give preference, not only for the manufacture of paper, but likewise for textile fabrics, ropes, sail-cloths, &c.

18. An indispensable factor in framing estimates *Cost of labour an important item in such estimates.* of agricultural operations is unquestionably the cost of labour, and the popular opinion that this is remarkably cheap in tropical countries often leads to false and untrustworthy calculations. I fear Mr. Routledge has fallen into this error when reducing his scheme to figures. Although many parts of India, and especially the

famine-stricken districts in the south, are over-populated, the reverse is often the case, as, for example, in Burma, which would be the chief seat of this new industry which Mr. Routledge advocates. There labour is exceedingly dear, a *coolie* commanding one rupee (say 1s. 10d.) per diem in the rice-shipping season, which is generally a busy time of the year with foresters. Moreover, as the people are physically weaker than Europeans, they do not turn out more than two-thirds of the work which the latter would perform in a day.

19. Another opinion which Mr. Routledge ex-presses is at variance with my experience, namely, that the bamboo "*will not only grow, but flourishes in localities unsuited for other cultivation*" (p. 36). Now I maintain that this is quite a wrong impression; indeed I would go further, and say, that all localities suited to the propagation of bamboo would, *cæteris paribus*, be equally well suited to the cultivation of almost any other crop. On the hill slopes, where—with the exception of *Bambusa spinosa* (which is confined to the plains, requiring deep alluvium near large rivers) all bamboos thrive best—during the annual fires, large quantities of bamboo are consumed with the other trees, and the land is afterwards cultivated with various crops. And in the plains the sites that would have to be selected for the development of Mr. Routledge's scheme (namely, lands situated on a stream containing water throughout the year) are precisely the localities which would at all times be

B

valuable for other cultivation. It must also be remembered, in passing, that, now that Government contemplates relieving India by encouraging emigration to Burma, land in that province will be still more valuable than it has hitherto been. To give

Difficulties in the way of trying Mr. Routledge's plan on the hills. Mr. Routledge's scheme a trial in the hills would, I fear, be quite impracticable ; firstly, because of the scantness of the highland population (there being hardly a sufficient number of men for our present timber operations), and, secondly, because of the scarcity of water at the season when the people of the plains might be employed without sacrifice of life from jungle fever, which the hill tribes are proof against.

20. Having thus completed my review of Mr. The author's proposals detailed. Routledge's proposition, I now proceed to detail my own views. I have already stated (paragraph 4) that in July, 1876, I submitted for the approval of the Chief Commissioner of British Burma, five specimens of paper. The first three of these were made from the fibre of three different varieties of the Ficus. These trees are valueless

The three varieties of Ficus valueless as timber. for timber, so that in utilizing their fibre we are turning to account a forest tree which flourishes abundantly in Burma, and which is capable of being propagated from slips or cuttings, the most simple and inexpensive mode of reproduction. These slips or cuttings are not mere twigs or tiny off-shoots, but huge limbs, seven or eight feet in length, and about two feet in circumference, indiscriminately cut or broken from the

parent tree. These boughs are simply *stuck* in the
No cultivation or care necessary. ground, and within twelve months they
become, without any further care or attention, well-
established, handsome young trees. In Burma,
many of the roads are avenued with this wide-
spreading tree, whose dense foliage renders it
peculiarly suited for the purpose.

21. The three samples of paper made from the
Paper manufactured of *Ficus* fibres pronounced excellent. fibre of these trees have been pronounced, by no less capable an au-
thority than Mr. Routledge, " excellent "; and, he
adds, that " if they bleach well and cheaply, retaining their strength, they will find a good market."
After such a favourable opinion from an experienced
paper-maker, I trust the authorities may think it
advisable to put the matter to the test of experiment,
and in the second part of this pamphlet I shall go
into the question of how this may most satisfactorily
be done. In the absence of trustworthy data, the
Primâ facie advantages of *Ficus* as compared with Bamboo. only apparent advantages that the
introduction of this paper-making
material offers us compared with bamboo, are that
(1) it can be produced at a lower cost; (2) it does
not require artificial irrigation ; and (3) its cultivation does not necessitate the appropriation of
land which could be turned to other account. The
valueless trees which abound in the forests of the
plains might, with great advantage, be made to
give room to different varieties of Ficus.

22. I venture to suggest that when the value of

The material should be imported in the form of "half-stock." this material is being tried, consignments of *half-stock* be imported, as the reduction of the fibre to this stage will be less costly, I imagine, than the manufacture of rough paper, which, at the best, would have again to be reduced to pulp before it would be of any service in the European paper market.

23.—I come now to the *fourth* of the five samples

The Author's fourth fibre, *Streblus aspera.* of paper, referred to in paragraph 20. This sample was manufactured from the fibre of *Streblus aspera*, an evergreen, from thirty to forty feet high, with clear stem from four to ten feet in length, and two and a-half to three feet in circumference. It is indigenous to Burma, and grows up to an elevation of 2000 feet. Not being able to give the exact cost of production, all I can do at present is to recommend it to fair trial, on the grounds that the paper made from it has been pronounced by experienced paper-makers of " excellent quality "; that it rapidly reproduces itself; that it abounds in the forests ; and that it is capable of being reproduced at a nominal cost, requiring neither artificial irrigation, nor any other expensive mode of treatment.

24. The remaining sample (the fifth) was made

The fifth fibre recommended by the Author, *Broussonetia papyrifera.* of the inner bark of *Broussonetia papyrifera*, a good coppicing plant capable of being propagated from cuttings, and indigenous to Burma. This sample has given universal satisfaction, and all experts in the paper trade unanimously acknowledge that the *Broussonetia papyrifera* is known to produce a first-class paper material,

and would find a very large sale if it could be produced at a remunerative price. There is nothing, so
far as I know, to prevent its successful introduction
into the market. Indeed, it seems wasteful to allow
so valuable an article to remain unused, the more so
as it is easily reproduced at comparatively small cost.
Besides being a valuable paper-yielding material,
the leaves of this plant afford good food for some of
the silk-worm family, so that the cultivation of the
Broussonetia papyrifera might be turned to a double
account; sericulture being an industry which already
engages the attention of the authorities in British
Burma.

25. There is another plant, the Calotropis
gigantea,* to which I would beg leave
to invite the special attention of the
Government of India, as affording one of the most pro-
mising fibre-yielding materials; while the method of
disengaging the fibre, as compared with the elaborate
processes attending the separation of all others,—
including jute, bamboo, flax, hemp, &c.—is so simple,
that the plant merits careful notice, as much on
grounds of economy as in consideration of the valuable quality of its fibre. The cost of production
might be materially decreased by substituting
machinery for the tedious method of separating the

Calotropis gigantea specially recommend- ed to the attention of Government.

* Common in most parts of India: shrub 6-10 feet; leaves stem-clasping,
decussate, oblong, ovate, wedge-shaped, bearded on the upper side at the
base, smooth on the upper surface, clothed with woolly down on the
under side; segments of corolla reflexed, with revolute edges, stameneous;
corona fine-leaved, shorter than the gynostegium; leaflets keel-formed,
circinately recovered at the base, incurved and subtridendate at the apex;
umbels sometimes compound, surrounded by involucral scales; follicles
ventricose, smooth, seeds comose; flowers rose-color and purple mixed.
Flowers all the year. NATURAL ORDER, Asclepiadaceæ.

Machine recommend-
ed for separation of
fibre.
fibre by manual labour, and I would recommend a simple machine (4-horse power) similar to that used in the manufacture of aloe-fibre, and capable of moving a pair of cylinders, on a system of beaters or stampers. To avoid delay, however, in making experiments with this plant, an improvement might be made on the rude mode of scutching, by introducing a common brake, consisting of four wooden swords fixed in a frame, and another frame with three swords which play into the interstices of the first series by means of a joint at one end. The final process prior to packing for export, can be easily and expeditiously accomplished by means of a board set upright in a block of wood, so as to stand firm. In this board is a longitudinal slit about three feet from the ground, the edge of which is thin. The broken fibre is inserted in the slit so as to project to the right, and with a flat wooden sword the fibre is repeatedly struck until all the pieces of wood which adhere to it are got rid of.

26. A still further saving might be effected by
Machine for com-
pressing the fibre
into bales.
compressing the fibres into bales by a simple hand machine* now in use among dealers in waste paper and others. The machine is capable of being worked by a man and a boy, who can turn out at the rate of 20 bales or two tons a day. The consignment might be shipped as ballast, as is now being done with the stalks of the maize from America.

* A drawing and estimate of a machine of this description was forwarded by me to the Commissioner in Sind last June.—G. W. S.

27. The Calotropis fibre has been pronounced by
Calotropis fibre equal to any and superior to most materials now in paper market. manufacturers of paper, rope, and textile fabrics equal to any fibre now in the market, and far superior to most of them ; and universal surprise has been expressed that so valuable an article should not have attracted public attention long ago. This fact is all the more astonishing when it is remembered that as far back as 1831 this valuable fibre was brought to the notice of the English public.

28. With such strongly-expressed professional
No reason why it should not be introduced. opinions in its favor, I think it can hardly be considered doubtful that there would be a demand for this fibre in the home market, and I see no reason why it should not be introduced with advantage to both buyer and seller. It is in all respects well-fitted to meet trade requirements, and, once introduced, there is nothing to prevent an enormous business in this fibre, a business far surpassing even that in jute. The fibre will be found to possess all those qualities which are requisite to produce a compact felted first-class paper ; namely, flexibility, strength, and length, it is also barbed and spiral, habits of growth that render flax more valuable for paper material than cotton.

29. The following information regarding this
Authority for following statements, plant is based on data obtained from the collector of Shikarpore, through Colonel Sir William Merewether, and may therefore be accepted as trustworthy.

30. One acre stocked with plants 4' × 4' would

Estimate of cost. equal 2704 plants; which will yield
582 pounds of *bonâ fide* fibre under the present rude
system of preparing it; or 727 pounds under a
more economical process, the waste in converting
the stalks into fibre being 25 per cent. That is to
say, this plant produces per acre nearly 6 cwt. more
fibre than cotton, the same amount as flax, and
only 47 lbs. less than hemp, and this too on land
absolutely valueless for any other crop. The yield of
stalks per acre has been estimated at about 10 tons.
The cost of cultivating one acre is fixed at £2 9s. 8d.;
but it must be borne in mind that when once this expenditure has been incurred, no further outlay will be
requisite. The Collector of Shikarpore,* however,
when referring to the plant in its wild state, writes :—
" There is enough growing wild to keep a dozen factories going ; the cultivation of the plant, therefore,
would perhaps be unnecessary. This officer further
gives it as his opinion that the plant is not ready for
cutting for two years if cultivated from seed; but
says that if cut down close to the ground, it grows
again rapidly, and would give a second crop within
twelve months of the first cutting. Colonel Sir William
Merewether, however, differs from the Collector as to
the time seedlings take to reach maturity. "The
only point " he says, " I do not agree with Colonel
Wallace on, is the time of growth of the plant. I re-
member once on the Noorwah near Jacobabad, water
was for the first time for years let over a piece of

---

* The Collectorate of Shikarpore merely embraces one of the five divi-
sions in the province of Sind ; the Calotropis growing in even more
prolific abundance in the remaining four collectorates.

ground. It (the water) happened to contain the seed of the *Calotropis*, and the consequence was the whole space was covered with *Calotropis* jungle close and six or seven feet high."*

31. The cost of manufacturing the fibre, which Cost of manufacture the only obstacle. is estimated at from £60 to £70 per ton, How to be overcome. is the only obstacle to its introduction into the market; but by utilizing the machine already referred to, this drawback might easily be overcome, and the Calotropis fibre prepared at about £7 per ton.

32. The following schedule gives the respective Schedule of prices of fibres not superior to Calotropis. current prices of the fibres which have been pronounced by experts not superior to that obtained from the Calotropis; it remains for Government to decide whether it is worth while to encourage a trade in this weed.

FIBRES.	RATE PER TON.			
		£		£
Jute	From	18	to	21
Sissil Hemp ..	,,	24	,,	32
Sun	,,	19	,,	26
Russian Hemp	,,	25	,,	32
Ditto Flax	,,	30	,,	43

* The Superintendent of Cotton Experiments in Sind, in a letter dated 15th November, 1877, writes :—"I do not think I could give you such an approximate estimate of the cost of bringing one acre of land under cultivation with *Calotropis*. It would not be much, as it is a weed here, and the difficulty is to prevent its taking possession of our fields to the exclusion of what are at present more valuable plants, and to my thinking, by the time any one requires to cultivate *UK* as an agricultural crop, the product may be safely left to take care of itself. In other words, before the available natural supply is insufficient to meet all demands, the article will have such a hold in the markets, both local and foreign, that those interested in its production may be safely left to deal with this as they see most likely to be to their advantage."

33. The question now arises whether the development of this trade should devolve on Government or whether it should be left entirely in the hands of the merchants, who might deal direct with the cultivators. Although, as a rule, Government monopolies are generally to be avoided, as interfering with trade principles, yet, in this particular instance, I cannot help thinking that this new industry would be most properly started by Government; for it must be borne in mind that this product is not a cultivated staple, but the natural produce of the soil, and, consequently, the legitimate property of the State. Another reason why Government should lay the foundation of this trade is, that it is already provided with the requisite materials to test the practicability and value of the industry at a minimum cost, while the merchant would have to incur a very large outlay before he could possibly arrive at any results, favourable or otherwise. This fact alone is sufficient to deter . many men from embarking in. a speculation of this nature, unless they have some substantial grounds for believing in ultimate success. It appears to me, in an undertaking of this nature, Government has everything to gain and nothing to lose, that it is hardly expedient to wait until mercantile enterprise develops the trade. If the merchant would increase his capital by opening out this new industry, Government would equally benefit by the enhancement of its revenue. If, then,

[marginal notes:]

Should the development of the industry be undertaken by Government or left to Merchants.

The plant is the legitimate property of the State.

Government has the requisite materials to test the suitability of the fibre for paper-making.

Government has everything to gain and nothing to lose in the matter.

Reasons for Government action as regards bamboo equally applicable to Calotropis. Government is willing to deal direct with paper-makers in the matter of bamboo, with how much more advantage might it take the initiative with regard to the Calotropis fibre. The same principle that applies to the development of trade in the one is equally applicable to the other, with this exception, perhaps, that while the Calotropis is a staple that has hitherto formed no part of trade, and will consequently never be originated by the natives who are at times unwilling to enter on a new line of agriculture; the bamboo has for years past been exported from the hills by the people, and sold in the markets on the plains. Certainly the matured stems are what have hitherto formed the trade, but in the same manner as the merchants in Burma arrange for the transport of timber from the hills, they might stipulate for succulent shoots of the bamboo being brought down, instead of matured stems. Again, as regards the cultivation of the two crops (Calotropis and bamboo), it appears to me that any reason for the Government objecting to undertake the culture of the one, applies with equal force in the case of the other; but in neither case can I see any valid reason why Government should refrain from laying the foundation of this new and important industry, ultimately relinquishing its right to import direct to the home market, but retaining its lien on the revenue of land that has hitherto been regarded as sterile and valueless.*

* The following extract will be found to support my views :—" The district officers, who have been consulted by the Commissioners, are unanimously of opinion that the production of fibres other than what are

These principles appear to be in accordance with the action the Government of India has recently taken for the development of a trade in rheea fibre.*

34. In further proof of the excellent quality of Author's sample of Calotropis fibre, so highly spoken of, was very inferior to what can be produced. the Calotropis fibre, I should mention that the sample which has been so favorably, reported on was very inferior compared with what the plant is capable of producing. In corroboration of this statement I give an extract from a letter received with the fibre :—

" In reply to your note about the *Calotropis* fibre, I beg to say that I will despatch to Kotree this evening 20 lbs. as requested. It is the produce of last season, or the newest that can be had just now. At present the Calotropis bark is too dry and woody; it will not strip at all ; or if any portion comes off, the fibre is scanty and very short. That sent you is about arm's length. The season for collecting the fibre is when the liber is soft, and the bark comes off clean and easily."

35. Further I would call attention to the fact, now already in the market, will not, and, considering their want of capital, cannot, be earnestly taken up by the cultivating classes in these provinces, until the presence of a real and permanent demand for them is generally known and felt. Indeed it is almost on all hands admitted that much valuable fibre, which might with little trouble and less cost be made suitable to the manufacture of paper, and even of cloth, is now absolutely wasted in all parts of the country from want of due attention and encouragement, and unless some impulse is given to the people, either by action of Government or private enterprise, it is hopeless to expect that the boundless supply of valuable fibres which the fertile soil of the country is perennially yielding will ever be utilized by local industry. When the industry is fully developed and appreciated by the agricultural classes the Government can easily withdraw from the field, leaving private enterprise to take its place."—*Report on the Cultivation of, and Trade in, Jute in Bengal, and on Indian Fibres available for the Manufacture of Paper.* By Hem Chunder Ker, Deputy Magistrate, on special duty to inquire into the production of, and trade in, Jute.

* *Vide* Government of India Notification No. 45, dated Simla, 31st of August, 1877.

Quality of fibre capable of being much improved. that the natural habit of growth of the Calotropis is not conducive to fine tall fibre, for the shrubs do not grow sufficiently near to one another. Thus the quality of the fibre is capable of being vastly improved by artificial cultivation.*

36. Manufacturers of paper appear generally to

The fibre of exogenous plants versus that of endogens, in connection with Calotropis. agree (on grounds of economy alone) that endogenous plants are better calculated to meet the requirements of the paper-trade than exogenous plants, the actual fibre yield of the latter being small as compared with that of the former, while the preparation of fibre from exogens is far more tedious and expensive than from endogens. This opinion, though as a rule correct, is hardly applicable to the Calotropis ; and as a set-off against the expenses attending the manipulation and growth of exogens for paper, it must be borne in mind that the Calotropis is a weed that flourishes on land that is absolutely unfitted for the growth or cultivation of any other crop, and, further, that it is independent of rain, or artificial irrigation, and that when once the seed is sown broadcast it requires no further atten-

* Without entering into the physiological structure of plants, it will sufficiently answer my purpose, and that of those whom this subject may interest, to briefly explain why plants growing at some distance apart will not yield so good a fibre as when they are grown close together. " The fibrous product of plants is only the woody fibre in a younger state, and may be considered as wood in a separated form, while wood may be described as consisting chiefly of amalgamated fibres. Exposure to light and air is well known to be essential to the formation of good wood, by favouring the proper secretions of the tree, and the thickening of the woody fibres. But this necessarily diminishes their flexibility, and therefore is not suited to plants which are grown on account of their fibres. Hence to obviate this undue exposure of the plants to light and air, and to favour their shooting upwards, and to prevent the formation of lateral branches, the seeds of both the hemp and the flax plant are sown thick in Europe, and the plants grown closer as the fibre is required to be finer." —*The Fibrous Plants of India.*—By D. Forbes Royle.—Smith, Elder & Co., London, 1855.

tion, continuing to reproduce itself after each successive cutting, *ad infinitum.*

37. I have already stated that the fibre of the Calotropis has been pronounced by experts capable of producing first-class paper ; and we may therefore fairly assume that it is superior to esparto, which, according to Mr. Arnott, " holds an intermediate place between cotton, flax, jute, and manilla, and those of wood and straw."* Now, according to the estimates of paper-makers, two tons of Spanish (at £10 per ton) are required to produce one ton of paper, and the cost of chemicals, fuel, labor, &c., per ton is £2 10s. : thus £25 may be accepted as the price of sufficient esparto to yield one ton of paper. From these figures a fair approximate, of the value of the *Calotropis* fibre may be arrived at ; and it must be remembered in framing this estimate, that the esparto is imported intŏ this country in the condition in which it is reaped, and that consequently the cost of reduction to pulp is enhanced. This reduces the yield per ton of paper-producing material 50 per cent.; while with the Calotropis the case is reversed, for the refuse combings will serve the purpose of paper-makers, and the longest staple will be available for manufacturers of rope, textile fabrics, &c. Moreover, as *bonâ fide* fibre is imported, the loss in conversion into paper-stock is reduced to a minimum.

38.—Apart from the fact that eventually the Calotropis must, if judiciously introduced, afford a material for paper, as good as, and cheaper than,

* " Canton Lectures," delivered before the Society of Arts.—By W. Arnott, F.L.S.

Threatened ex-
haustion of sup-
ply of esparto. esparto, the rapid exhaustion of this sedge is threatened by the improvident method of plucking up roots and all, resorted to by the natives of Spain, while *Alfa* (or African esparto), which is also used for paper, realizes a much lower price, being in all respects, I believe, inferior to the Spanish,—indeed it is, I am told, chiefly employed as a blend.

39.—I will now pass on to the next subject that Utilization of plants hitherto regarded as evils. appears to me worthy of consideration, —I mean the utilization of certain plants which have hitherto been regarded as evils, which must be got rid of at any price.

40.—How to suppress the annual jungle-fires The annual jun- gle-fires ; their suppression a serious problem. has ever been, and will, I fear, long re- main, one of the greatest problems to be solved by Indian Foresters. Various and numerous have been the remedies resorted to, at very heavy expenditure, and without any benefit, except, perhaps, the partial control of the conflagrations for one or more seasons.

41.—These fires generally occur between March The jungle-fires. and May, when the whole vegetation of the country is parched and dried up from the severe droughts at this season. The jungles are then fired by the people, with the double object of securing a fresh crop of succulent grass for their cattle on the first burst of the rains, and of facilitating their moving about the country with less risk of death by reptiles and wild beasts. It sometimes so happens, perhaps, that these conflagrations are caused by the friction of trees, but this is certainly the exception.

42.—To prevent these fires extending to our State
Forests, these are surrounded by roads,
with an intermediate belt of high forest,
which is intended to check the spread of sparks;
the inner cordon is 100 yards wide, and the outer
25 yards, both being cleared of high coarse grass
and other vegetation. It often happens, however,
that even this precaution is insufficient, for the fires,
fanned by the high winds which prevail at this time
of the year, travel with such rapidity and fierceness,
that the tongue of flame leaps over the outer road,
and, setting fire to the fallen dead leaves in the
intermediate belt of forest, ultimately even crosses
the inner *fire-trace*, and baffles the efforts of the fire-
watchers to extinquish it. As a remedy for this (it
being found impracticable to keep the intermediate
strips of jungle free of fallen leaves), an excellent
suggestion was made by my native overseer just
before I left Burma, namely, to plant the strip of
jungle with pine-apples, which are known to thrive
best under wide-spreading trees; and there is no
doubt that if the fibre of these plants, which is of
very superior quality,* were turned to account, the
system would be doubly beneficial.†

43.—In speaking of the utilization of materials at

* "Average weight sustained by slips of paper in the water-leaf, or un-
sized condition, each weighing 39 grains, 71 lbs. Average weight sustained by slips of paper of 39 grains, after being sized, 74¼ lbs. Worked
very "wet" in pulping. Makes a good and very strong paper."—Report
on Rheea Fibre, by J. Forbes Watson, M.A., M.D., LL.D., &c., Reporter
on the Products of India.

† It has always been a matter of surprise to me that a company for the
distillation of pine-apple wine, or spirit, has never been started in Burma,
when this fruit in the season can be purchased at the rate of two for a
penny.

present regarded as an evil, I refer more particularly Grass Fibres. to the conversion of the high grasses into fibre that might be imported into Europe in this form, or in that of *half-stock*, whichever, after trial, proved the more profitable form for shipment. And I would beg leave at this point to remind the Authorities that the same machine which is suited for the manufacturing of the *Calotropis* fibre is equally well adapted to the manufacture of the grass fibre. Further on I shall have occasion to refer to these grasses again, and I shall then enumerate the parts of India where they abound, and where they so seriously interfere with the forest conservancy. I shall also give my authority for stating that they are peculiarly adapted to the requirements of the paper and rope trade, being light, tenacious, and capable of bearing, without injury, alternate exposure to wet and dry. At this stage of my argument I shall confine myself to stating the probable yield of grass per acre, and the cost of its conversion into fibre.

44. One acre of land has been estimated to yield Estimated yield of grass-fibre and cost of preparation. 15,375 lbs., or nearly 7 tons of unhandled raw material, and 62 per cent. of *bonâ fide* manufacture, averaging from 2 to 2½ feet long, at a cost of £3 17s. The grass is irrepressible, and will yield a second crop of fibre within twelve months of the first cutting; it is independent of irrigation other than the annual inundations, and it requires no cultivation. It seems clear, then, that by turning this grass to account we should not only be bene-

c

fiting our forests, but also enhancing the revenue of
India from a hitherto waste product. At the same
time we should accomplish the different objects for
which the people at present find it necessary to
resort to, the extermination of the grasses by fire.
I venture to hope that the figures I have given are
sufficiently plain to induce the Government to direct
that a consignment of *Sur** be imported to England.
The prospect is very encouraging for those who
choose to embark in new undertakings for the supply
of commercial fibres. The plant grows wild on the
banks of rivers ; there is every facility for cheap
exports; and if the simple machine which I have
recommended for Calotropis fibre be substituted for
manual labour the value of the product would be
materially increased.

45. Another branch of forest conservancy, of no
Fibre obtainable from creepers, removal of which is an important branch of forest conservancy. less importance than the suppression of
fires, is the removal from trees of the
gigantic creepers which twine round and
ultimately kill them. Now, many of the creepers
yield most excellent fibre,—that of the *Bauhinia varie-*
Bauhinia variegata. *gata*, for example, which overruns our forests,
having been pronounced by paper-makers equal to
the fibre of *Adansonia digitata,* which is known to
afford a very superior material for paper. So again
Butea frondosa and B. superba. with the Butea frondosa and B. superba,
which grow in equal abundance, and from which
strong ropes are made ; and there are many others,

* *Saccharum munja.* Culms straight, eight to twelve feet, smooth ;
leaves channelled, long, linear, white-nerved, hispid at the base inside ;
panicles large, oblong, spreading ; ramifications verticelled ; flowers
hermaphrodite ; corolla two-valved.

Chavannesia esculenta. among which must be numbered Chavannesia esculenta.* Now, if the creepers that have annually to be cut down were converted into fibre and shipped to Europe, a large revenue would result from what it has cost us hitherto a considerable amount to clear away. Here again is a subject which challenges our careful consideration.

46. Before concluding the first section of my pamphlet, I would desire to draw prominent attention to one more valuable fibrous plant, and I take the opportunity of saying, in passing, that I have by no means exhausted the stock at our disposal.

Many more valuable fibrous plants besides those mentioned.

47. All who are familiar with the varied and profuse vegetation of Burma must have observed the prolific growth of the wild plantain throughout the province, most, if not all the forests being clothed with a sub-arborescent growth of this magnificent herbaceous plant, whose stems are formed partly of the united petioles of the leaves, charged with spiral vessels. These are capable of being disengaged abundantly, yielding strong filaments, which are of a silky silvery white, and retain their lustre even after they are dyed. The fibre of this plant is not only valuable for paper, but likewise for light fabrics, the finer sorts of furniture hangings, damask, upholstery, &c.†

Fibre of wild plantain, strong and silky, and retains lustre after dyeing.

* Note on Caoutchouc obtained from the Chavannesia esculenta.—By G. W. Strettell. Government Printing Press, Rangoon, 1874.

† Last May I drew Mr. Routledge's attention to this fibre, and I believe a small sample consignment has recently been sent to him from Burma. It is not at all improbable that the cost of preparing the fibre has far exceeded its market value, but this should not discourage the authorities, nor lead to the abandonment of the enterprise, for it must be remembered that first experiments are always expensive, especially when conducted by inexperienced hands.

48. The following extract, taken from an essay

Plantain fibre compared with other fibres. by Mr. P. S. Simmonds, will give a clear idea of the relative value of plantain fibre and other kinds. Referring to cotton, the author writes :—" It is subject to many deteriorating influences, particularly from frost or excessive rain ; and a full average crop is considered to be one bale per acre, or about four cwt. Flax, also an annual, is regarded as a good crop at six cwt. per acre, and hemp at seven cwt. per acre. The plantain will yield, of the best quality of fibre, 48 cwt. per acre, besides the coarser qualities, consequently its produce will be, as compared with that of cotton, twelve-fold ; of flax, eight-fold ; and of hemp, seven-fold. Moreover, the produce of the plantain from 500 acres would require to obtain the same quantity in cotton, 6,000 acres, in flax 4,000, and in hemp 3,500 acres. But flax and hemp being exhausting crops cannot be grown on the same land oftener (at the utmost) than in a five year rotation ; therefore, to produce annually, for seven years, 1,200 tons of flax would require the use of an estate of 20,000 acres ; and for hemp, in the same way, 17,500 acres. But the plantain not being an exhausting crop would continue to produce its 1200 tons of fibre per annum, without replanting for a term of twelve or fifteen years about 500 acres."

End of Part I.

PART II.

The suitability of the fibre-yielding plants of India
Introductory. for the manufacture of textile fabrics and
paper has so repeatedly formed the subject of inquiry,
that I can say little that is new on the matter. In
the collision of many opinions, however, truth must
ultimately be established, and the wider and more
thorough the investigation, the more rapidly and
certainly will the truth be reached.

2. One of the principal reasons why the fibres of
Energetic practical measures essential. India have not come into universal favor
is that their importance has not been seriously real-
ized, and that their introduction has not been urged
with sufficient emphasis. Until the question is dealt
with in an earnest and practical manner no successful results can be looked for. It is not enough to
forward, for the opinion of Chambers of Commerce
and Brokers, small samples of such new materials as
from time to time attract the attention of intelligent
observers. Such steps seldom lead to any practical
results, and the matter is too often lost sight of, until
at some future time the subject is revived by an
enterprising enquirer. It is because of the deep
interest I take in the opening out of the fibre trade

of India, and because I· am convinced that an energetic and thorough enquiry into the subject will
result in a great gain to the revenue of that country,
that I have written this essay in the interests of the
Government whose servant I am.

3.   There is at present an increasing demand for
cheap material for paper-making, and the
opportunity seems favorable for the investigation of the whole question of the importance, alike
to the Government and the consumer, of these great
sources of wealth, which have so long remained in-
sufficiently appreciated in the European markets, and
valueless commodities to our Eastern Dependencies.
At a time when it is necessary to borrow eight and
a-half millions to defray the expenses of famine relief,
and when the future of the silver question is wholly
uncertain, the importance of developing
every source of wealth must be apparent,
and although our endeavours in connection with
Indian fibres have hitherto been futile, there is every
reason to hope that, if the work is wisely taken in
hand, the efforts of the Government will yet be
crowned with success.   I, of course, perfectly appreciate the necessity for railroads and canals, but these
are costly, and not always—perhaps not generally—
remunerative undertakings, and I would respectfully
and strongly urge upon the Government of India
the advisability of utilizing the thousands of acres of
sterile land which might be cultivated with
a crop absolutely independent of rain or
artificial irrigation, and which thrives with a mini-

Marginal notes:

Present time specially suit- able for this enquiry.

Importance, at present, of de- veloping every source of wealth.

Crop indepen- dent of rainfall or irrigation.

mum of water.* If only a fraction of the expenditure necessary to relieve the distress of famine-stricken districts were devoted to the industry I am advocating, not only would India's revenue be increased, but the condition of her population would be transformed from one of poverty to independence, and India would no longer be compelled to appeal to England in time of famine. As Mr. Bright remarked in his speech at the opening of the Manchester Town Hall: "Almsgiving on behalf of Indian sufferers is most commendable, still it will do little for the future." A source of wealth is at our doors if we will only learn how to utilize it.

4. A study of the physical geography of India—its soil and climate—shows that it can afford an unfailing supply of fibre much superior *(cæteris paribus)* to any that can be produced by any other country. In proof of this fact, Mr. Dickson, writing to the *Journal of the Society of Arts*,† refers the public, by way of challenge, to his own collection, and that exhibited at the East India House. It is, indeed, undeniable that, in addition to the materials at present in use for the manufacture of paper and textile fabrics, there are many fibres available for the same purpose, and I hope to prove

India can produce better fibres than any other country.

---

* Speaking at Bradford, in October last, the Marquis of Salisbury remarked in connection with the fallacy of supposing that a vast system of irrigation would prove an effectual remedy against famine:—"If famine only came in regions where irrigation is physically possible, the remedy might be applicable. But, unfortunately, the native population, in reliance on the annual rains, spreads over districts where irrigation is not possible, because there are no great rivers from which to take the water, and no plains over which to conduct it."

† "The Fibrous Plants of India," page 132.—By J. Forbes Royle, M.D., F.R.S.—Smith, Elder & Co., 1855.

that the one I am most in favor of can be introduced into the European markets at a saleable price.

5. Some idea may be obtained of the expanse of The size of territory on which we can rely for a constant supply of fibres by a study of the map of India. Its extreme length from Cape Comorin to Cashmere is about 2000 miles, and its greatest breadth from the bend of the Burrampootra to the mouths of the Indus must be nearly as great, but from its irregular figure the superficial area is only estimated at 1,500,000 square miles. It is bounded on the N.W. by the Indus, and on the N.E. by the Himalayan Mountains, while the Indian Ocean washes its remaining sides; the whole forming a kind of irregular diamond, to which the island of Ceylon forms a pendant.

6. Singular as it may appear, it is nevertheless India and China long known as true, that although the records of the past fibre - producing countries. have pointed to India and China as pre-eminently lands of fibres, these are the last two countries we have looked to for supplies, and no endeavour has been made to stimulate a trade with them. The art of paper-making from unwoven fibres appears to date from 95 A.D., when the Chinese first discovered the process of reducing raw fibre to pulp in water. From that time to the present day these intelligent people have continued to improve in the art, and now utilize various woven and unwoven materials, including cotton, rags, rice, straw, *Broussonetia papyrifera*, and bamboo (both the matured stems and the young shoots).

7. Although the precise date at which paper was
The Indians early acquainted with weaving. first manufactured in India does not
appear to be known, yet according to
Mr. Yates' *Textrinum Antiquorum* it seems that
when the inhabitants of Europe and Western Asia
were clothed in skins and furs, the Chinese wore silk,
and the Indians garments made from a downy substance obtained from trees. At a still earlier period
the natives of India were acquainted with the art of
spinning and weaving, as we learn from their Vedas;
while in the Institutes of Menu, written 800 years B.C.,
we read that the sacrificial thread of a Brahmin must
be of cotton, that of a Kshatriya of *sana* thread
only, and that of a Vaisya of woollen thread. It is
evident, therefore, that even at those remote periods
the natives of India utilized their indigenous fibres,
and it is not improbable that the manufacture of
paper soon followed the art of weaving, and that the
people of India did not long remain content with
palm leaves, bark, stones, &c., to write on. However
this may be, there is abundant proof of the prolific
yield of fibrous material in India. This is now
largely used for paper-making throughout the Empire, and I have myself seen paper being made in the
most remote parts of Burma Proper from wild-grow-
ing fibres common to the district. The process is
described in the "Narrative of my Journey in search
of the *Ficus elastica.*"*

* "The Ficus Elastica in Burma Proper; or, a Narrative of my Journey in Search of it, &c., &c."—By G. W. Strettell, Government Press,
Rangoon, 1876.

8. Long prior to the publication of Forbes Royle's Early writers on Indian fibres. exhaustive work on the fibrous plants of India,* published in 1855, other writers had from time to time called public attention to the merits of our tropical fibres, and the facility with which they are to be obtained. On the death of Dr. Roxburgh, his valuable correspondence on this subject was published in a volume, entitled, " *Observations, &c., on the various specimens of Fibrous Vegetables and produce of India which may prove valuable substitutes for hemp and flax some future day in India.*" From 1806 we continue to read of specimens of fibres from India being forwarded for examination and report; and a large assortment was shewn at the London Exhibition of 1851. Since then, up to the present time, sample consignments have frequently been imported in the hope of attracting the attention of manufacturers of paper, cordage and textile fabrics. Singularly enough, however, with the exception of coir, jute, Rheea, and perhaps one or two others, the fibres of India continue to form no part of European commerce.

9. This state of things cannot, as I have shewn, Why Indian fibres, with a few exceptions, form no part of European commerce. be attributed to want of information. It is rather, I think, due to unwillingness on the part of importers to deal with new commodities, and partly also, no doubt, to the fact that Government has, for various reasons, been unable to devote serious attention to the matter.

* " The Fibrous Plants of India," by D. Forbes Royle.—Smith, Elder and Co., London, 1855.

10. The history of the esparto and jute trade, Every new article of trade must first be fairly tried. and indeed the history of every great trade which has succeeded in establishing itself, affords ample confirmation of the truth of what I have said. All experience goes to shew that for a new article of commerce even to find a sale—not to speak of its realizing its true value—it must have been first tried and approved.

11. Although paper made from esparto was The history of esparto an illustration. shewn at the Exhibition of 1851, this fibre remained unappreciated for several years, although at that time paper-making materials were sufficiently scarce to excite public anxiety, and to attract the attention of the Lords Commissioners of Her Majesty's Treasury, who deputed Dr. Royle in 1854 to consider the matter, and, if possible, to suggest some new substance that would be likely to prove suitable. I am also informed by Mr. Thomas Routledge that, although his first patent was dated 1856, and he was daily making printing paper of fair quality and selling it in the market, yet it was only in 1861, when the American War threatened a cotton famine, that this sedge gained notoriety, and then, he says, he could not import a sufficient quantity. In his interesting pamphlet on "Bamboo as a Paper Material," he writes : "The importations of esparto, which did not amount to 1000 tons in the year 1860 (indeed up to that date I was the only manufacturer using it), rose to upwards of 50,000 tons in the year 1865 ; and by 1871—ten years only from its introduction— the annual imports have attained the large total of

140,000 tons." So likewise with jute. On its introduction it had a hard struggle for existence, and I have been told that it was at first pronounced by certain spinners to be only fit to make rope to hang the introducers. The Crimean War, threatening scarcity of flax and hemp, changed the tide of affairs, and caused a great run on jute. Yet the exports in 1857 amounted to only 18 tons, valued at £62. At present, next to rice, jute is the chief staple of Bengal, and, exclusive of gunny bags, the average quantity exported annually amounted to 7,000,000 cwt., valued at four and a-half millions sterling. In a Blue Book,* published by the India Office in 1874, I find that France took in 1872-73 148,876 cwt. direct from Calcutta, and 550,000 cwt. from England ; Trieste took 9,000 cwt. direct from India; and Holland received 5,357 cwt. from India, and 58,610 cwt. from England. In 1872 Germany took 77,831, Belgium 31,192, Spain 20,768, and other countries 16,176 cwt. *viâ* England.

12. The history of the Rheea trade is not less interesting. The quality of the fibre, which was known to be far superior to any other, and for which there was an unlimited demand, at prices varying from £50 to £70 per ton, was brought to the notice of Government as far back as 1811. A Government has many things to think of, and it was not until some 58 years had elapsed that decisive

The history of Rheea another illustration.

* Statement, exhibiting the Moral and Material Progress and Condition of India during 1872-73. Ordered by the House of Commons to be printed 2nd June, 1874.

measures were adopted to open up a trade in this
fibre. The difficulty of separating the fibre and bark
from the stem had always stood in the way, manual
labour having been found too laborious to make the
cultivation on a large scale pay. In 1869 Government resolved to overcome the difficulty, and two
prizes were offered for the best and second best
machine for manufacturing Rheea fibre at £15 a ton,
which should fetch in the market a price averaging
£50 per ton. Owing, perhaps, to the cost and risk
attending the transport of machinery to India, or
for other reasons, only one person ventured to
compete. His machine was not altogether a
success; but in consideration of its being a *bond fide*
attempt he was awarded £1,500. Since then, more
progress seems to have been made, although I gather
from the following extract, taken from the *Overland
Mail* of June last, that the trade in this fibre is not
so brisk as it should be : " It does not seem," says
the writer, " that the progress in Rheea cultivation in
India, though very rapidly increasing, keeps pace with
the demand. The value has more than doubled in
the course of a year, and we learn from brokers who
are on the look-out for shipments that there is nothing to be gained by making much of Rheea in their
circulars, as there are no supplies at present
available."

13. The ill success which has hitherto attended
Paralyzing effect our efforts to utilize the fibre-producing
of the failure of
efforts hitherto plants of India has doubtless had a
made.
paralyzing influence, and fostered the belief that

nothing more remains to be done in this direction; but I sincerely trust that the Government will not give way to any such feeling of despair. The difficulties connected with the manufacture of Rheea fibre do not exist in the case of the plants which I am advocating, and I am convinced that a fair trial will show that we have at our feet in India an easily manageable source of wealth.

14.—It cannot be too distinctly stated, however, *Energy and enterprize essential to success.* that energy and enterprize are essential to success in this undertaking as in all others. We must begin with a firm determination to overcome first difficulties if we are desirous of ascertaining the great intrinsic value of our Eastern fibres. How to set to work is a very serious and important question. It is hopeless to depend entirely or principally on brokers, for they are not, as a rule, experts in any particular branch of trade, but base their valuations on speculative data, which, at the best, are liable to great fluctuation. The way which *The preliminary step to be taken.* seems to me best, is to enlist the services and co-operation of a substantial firm in the trade, who will undertake to institute themselves agents, in consideration of certain concessions to be guaranteed to them. I should suggest that, with a view to carrying out this idea, the Government should start with the understanding that they must be prepared at the outset to make a sacrifice, in the hope of ultimate gain, and supply the sample consignment (which, I may venture to say, in passing, should in no case be under five tons), for experiment, free of

charge.* If, after trial, the fibre is found to answer,
it may perhaps be requisite to make a still further
sacrifice, and supply the market at cost price; but
such a measure would be exceptional and of brief
duration, for the law of supply and demand would
soon fix the value of the commodity, and the trade
would then become established. The principle in-
volved in this proposal is one of such universal application in Commerce that it is, I presume, unnecessary to offer any arguments in its defence.

15. Royle, in his work already referred to, when
Royle on the dif-
ficulty of intro-
ducing new arti-
cles of trade.
dwelling on the difficulty of introducing a
new article into the market, says :—" The
only mode of ascertaining the value of a fibre or any
other product is to see what it will bring in the open
market. This is, no doubt, true of such articles as
are known; but if a new product is sent into the
market few of the regular purchasers will buy it, as
they want that to which their machinery and manufacturers are suited. I am told that it is only by
sending an article for some years into market that it
attracts attention. When worked up and found
useful, inquiries are subsequently made for it, and by
degrees its properties are determined and its real
value ascertained, as we may see on examining the

* This quantity will be found to be none too much for practical purposes,
for although microscopic investigation will no doubt decide the merits of
fibres hereafter, at present manufacturers require that they be put to the
experimentum crucis before they will become purchasers. Mr. Thos. Routledge, referring to a sample of fibre that was sent to him, writes : " The
small quantity of Musa I received (a few lbs. only) is wholly insufficient
for practical experiment With two tons I might do something, although
not much, as the yield of the dried crushed stems would not be more
than 35 per cent., and we boil one ton at a time. You will see, therefore, that two tons leaves no margin for experimenting."

present and former comparative prices of jute. * * * * * * * The difficulty in making new things known and appreciated as articles of commerce arises chiefly from the habitual neglect of such things when sent for inquiry from abroad, in order to have their value ascertained at home; for if sent as specimens, I have seen many reports in which they are pronounced to be of NO VALUE because they are UNKNOWN IN THE MARKET. The importer is sometimes advised to send the article in large quantities to the market for a few years, as it will then have a chance of being looked at, and its true value ascertained. The planter is not often inclined to follow this advice; for if one more adventurous than his neighbours does send a quantity sufficient even for manufacturing purposes, it is not usually brought to the notice of the more enquiring manufacturers. The article being necessarily consigned by the planter to his agents, is by them transferred to a broker, by whom it is sold, with other colonial produce, with little or no information respecting its properties or the quantities in which, and the price at which, it could be supplied, if it should be approved of. Indeed, I am informed that the novelty of the appearance, or the strangeness of the name, is more often the subject of jest, than the article is one of serious inquiry. At all events, the result usually is, that the article is sold at a price which does not pay its expenses, and the planter is deterred from sending any fresh quantities. Further progress is, in that quarter at least, thus stopped even at its commencement."

16. Hitherto I have expressed the opinions of
The Author's experiences. others regarding the difficulty attending
the introduction of new articles into the market, however valuable they may be. I now propose to give my
own experience. Shortly after my return from India
(on two years' furlough) in September, 1876, I turned
my attention to the development of a trade in the
Indian fibres, which I had with me ; and with this
end in view I circulated among the leading manufacturers of paper and rope samples, with detailed
information respecting them, requesting an opinion
on their quality, and tenders for consignments should
they meet with approval. Without exception the
replies were satisfactory in the extreme. The manufacturers were unanimous in their praise, but though
loud in encomiums, pronouncing the fibres fit for
first-class paper, textile fabrics, and rope manufacture, no one seemed willing to make a *bonâ fide* offer,
each apparently wishing some one else to make the
first trial before speculating himself.

17. At that time I had not read Dr. Royle's work,
The Author's experiences continued. and I could not understand how it was
that all were so slow to seize so valuable
an opportunity, especially at a time when the high
price of paper, &c., was maintained by a scarcity of
the raw material. Though somewhat disheartened I
was determined to unravel the mystery, and finding
more was to be done by personal interview than by
correspondence I resolved to adopt the former
course. I soon found that the difficulty to be overcome was a stubborn belief that if India possessed

D

such valuable fibres as I exhibited, and was capable of importing them in sufficient quantities, and at remunerative prices, it was impossible that the trade should not have established itself long ago. It appeared hopeless to disabuse men of this belief, although I did my utmost to strengthen my views by arguments based on past experience.*

18. After the expenditure of much labor, time, and money, I ultimately persuaded one firm in the wholesale trade to give the fibres a fair trial. They were careful to protect themselves from any serious loss, though their terms were, I must acknowledge, extremely liberal, and all that could be expected at this stage of the undertaking. Indeed, had they not come forward as pioneers my efforts must have fallen through, unless Government had felt inclined to once more test the pulse of the market through the medium of the brokers.†

The Author's experiences continued. The first step gained.

19. The conditions on which the firm I allude to agreed to introduce the fibres were (1) that Government should supply them with a sample consignment of 15 tons *gratis*, the freight on

The Author's experiences continued.

---

* Thirty-four years ago no doubt the same objection would have been raised to the cultivation of cinchona and tea in India, yet both are now established crops, growing abundantly. For the former we are indebted to the energy of Mr. Clements Markham, and for the latter to the enterprise of the late East India Company, for although during its rule it reaped no immediate benefit from the liberal experiments it made at a great sacrifice, yet in subsequent years the exports of tea amounted to one and a-half million pounds, valued at £153,000, and although one single province, Assam, now rivals China, the trade may still be regarded as in its infancy. In the Western Dooars the cultivation of tea has been but little developed, though that district is spoken of as peculiarly adapted to the growth of this plant.

† I have already said that I do not consider this a satisfactory or fair way of testing the market. Moreover, the costs attending such sales generally swallow up the whole of the profits.

which they were willing to pay. In the event of the
fibre turning out of use, they further demanded (2)
a concession of 3,000 tons at a fair market valuation,
provided such price proved profitable to both parties.
With regard to the rough papers referred to in the
first part of this pamphlet (page 8), the same firm
agreed (3) to test their value, if samples of not less
than two tons of each kind were sent to them free of
all cost, and to become purchasers if the material
could be utilized in the paper-trade, and the price
fixed by Government was not prohibitory. These
terms by no means imply an entire control or monopoly of the trade, for so soon as the fibres became
known, the law of supply and demand would deter-
mine their real value, and thus the trade would be
placed in the best possible ground for insuring ultimate success. This prospect of future gain has induced me to recommend to the local administrations
of Sind and Burma that the foregoing terms be accepted, and I trust both Her Majesty's Secretary of
State for India and the Government of India will ap-
prove of the measures I have adopted.*

20. For over a century efforts have been made
Many fibre yield-
ing plants, but
few of them will
pay. from time to time to reduce the cost of
paper by the introduction of a cheaper
raw material. In the British Museum may be found
a record of 60 different specimens of paper, manufactured as far back as 1772. These experiments go
to prove that while the number of fibre-yielding

* *Vide* Appendix.

plants is legion, that the number of plants yielding fibre of commercial value is small.

21. The following, then, are the conditions upon *Necessary conditions to induce paper-makers to purchase.* which paper-makers require to be satisfied, before they will be induced to become purchasers of a new material, and importers should bear these conditions in mind when estimating the value of their produce. (1) * The fibre must be superior, or equal, to that already in the market, and the price at which it can be sold must be sufficiently low to leave a margin for profit to the buyer and manufacturers. (2) A constant and uniform supply, not liable to any sudden or great fluctuation in price, must be guaranteed.

22. The next point of importance is the prepara-*The preparation of the fibre. Importance of machinery.* tion of the fibre, and on this great care must be bestowed. Mechanical aid will ensure economy, and no time should be lost in securing the best appliances. Greed of gain often leads to quality being disregarded for quantity, and thus it happens that, for want of care in the manufacture of the article, its price falls in the home market, and the province whence it is imported gets a bad name, although the only fault is carelessness in the manipulation of the raw material.† As a further proof of this, let us contrast the result of our experi-

* *Vide* Appendix.

† As an example of this, Mr. P. S. Simmons in " *British Manufacturing Industries* " tells us, that " the unskilfully prepared Bombay hemp is found to be much less enduring than that from Madras and Bengal, and on this account rope made from it is carefully avoided by all first-class ship-chandlers." Here we have a striking instance, if not of absolute ignorance, certainly of neglect ; and there is little doubt that the absence of skilled labour in dealing with our raw produce has in many cases detracted from its market value.

ments in tobacco culture with those made in France—where the plant is a State monopoly. While with us the matter is still under enquiry, in France the scheme has been fully matured, and the result is a revenue about equal to that which we derive from opium. Why should this be, when we have soil in our favour, and when India carried off the first medal at the Paris Exhibition of 1867 ? Doubtless we have had many other prominent questions to occupy our attention, but this has now become as important as any of them. In France the same pains are taken in the selection of seed and soil as with the final preparation of the leaf; and this branch of agriculture forms a distinct department, managed by a corps of trained men from the Ecole Polytechnique. If we are equally careful in the manufacture, and if it be placed on a satisfactory financial footing, I confidently predict that fibre will form an item in the revenue of India not less important than iron, coal, silk, cotton, and tobacco, each of which has in turn been held up as a main-spring of the future wealth of the country. The dimensions to which this industry may attain will be understood when I state that there are 812 paper-mills in Great Britain and Ireland. One paper-maker alone (according to his own statement) consumes at the rate of 120 tons a week; and I have been told that the mills of the *Daily Telegraph* consume about 80 tons a month. The number of distinct trades wholly dependent on paper are 24—while there are numerous others which are chiefly supported by it.

23.   Under ordinary circumstances we expect the

people of a country to be alive to their own interests, and to develop their own resources, the Government if necessary taking the part of Instructor.   This acknowledged principle, sound as it no doubt is, cannot, however, be extended to India, for although telegraphs and steam communication have done much towards enlightening the people of the Eastern world, and raising them a stage higher in the scale of civilization, it is a mistake to suppose that the natives of India are sufficiently advanced to be altogether out of leading-strings, or that the development of agricultural industries can be entirely entrusted to them. There is, perhaps, no more improvident and less enterprising race in the world.   They are content with the small returns afforded by the means of livelihood handed down by their ancestors, and this is one of the reasons why they are less able to face a failure of crops than the European labourer.   In India, a bad harvest simply implies absolute starvation; whereas in England a similar adversity—which is of no uncommon occurrence—merely demands the abandonment of luxuries, not of the necessaries of life.   For this unsatisfactory state of affairs there are two chief reasons.   In the first place, the natives of India live literally from hand to mouth, and leave no margin for unforeseen vicissitudes common to all countries; and, secondly, they do not turn to the greatest advantage the whole of the land at their disposal.   The rapid strides which education is making in India will no doubt do much to work a reform, and when the natives learn to feel that every new hand is an additional source of wealth, and to appreciate the fact that the earth has treasures for him who will dig, we need not trouble ourselves about Indian famines. In the meantime Government has done much to check depopulation, by the suppression of disease, blood-feuds, wars, raids, infanticide, *suttie*, and other devastating influences ; and the practical result of all this is that more employment and more food must be found for the fast increasing population of our Eastern Empire.

24. It is extremely difficult to draw the line
The Government stands in loco parentis to the natives. where the parental interference of Government is to end; experience is the only guide. Habitual lethargy and fatalism have hitherto retarded progress, and induced the people of India to be content with their present frugal mode of existance ; while ignorance in like manner has led them to believe that none but the more fertile plains, which are subject to periodical rains or other modes of irrigation, can be turned to account. But among the multitude there are perhaps a few to be found more intelligent than the rest, and willing to benefit by instruction and advice, but who are unable, owing to want of means and guidance, to venture on speculations involving a large outlay of capital.

25. Government might probably, with advantage,
Danger of being dependent on one crop. step in here, and by example show the value of interchange of commerce and the

folly of being satisfied with the mere supply of immediate wants. Another lesson, which it is of the greatest importance the natives of India should learn, is that which we are taught by the great Potato Blight of 1845-1847, namely, the inadvisability of being entirely dependent on one crop, which at the best is at all times liable to failure, when there is another staple equally lucrative, that grows on the most sterile soil, and which, if not entirely independent of rain or artificial irrigation, flourishes with an infinitesimal amount of humidity—and is not liable to blight or other causes of failure common to vegetable life. I have particularly in my mind the *Calotropis*, The *Calotropis gigantea.* a perennial plant whose fibre is scarcely equalled, and which reproduces itself from the stool within twelve months of the first cutting. It grows all over India, though flourishing best in a dry climate and in sandy deserts, and is not killed or stunted by drought. It has been described by one writer in the following terms :—" The *Calotropis gigantea* grows all over India; it seems to thrive on soils that either destroy or reject everything else. It is difficult to conceive anything less productive than dry sand, yet the *Calotropis* thrives in it. Should its cotton be found useful, the waste lands of India could be covered with it, as it requires no culture."* When the writer gave expression to these views, he was evidently not aware of the valuable fibre-yielding properties of the plant, and merely referred to the

* Mr. Moncton, page 307. Royle's " Fibrous Plants of India."

downy substance contained in the follicles. This is, however, the least important part of the plant, though far from valueless ; for Dr. Royle tells us it has been found, when mixed with one-fourth of cotton, to produce a capital cloth, that stands washing, and takes a dye well. Another writer describes this plant as follows :—" The *Calotropis gigantea (ákanda*, commonly called *mudár*, sanskrit arká), is a valuable medicinal plant, and is largely used in Indian pharmacy. It grows wild on arid wastes, rubbish mounds, and other neglected places, whence it is collected for its milky juice, seeds, and flossy seed covering. The first two products are used in medicine, and the last for the decoration of toys. The fibre prepared from its bark is of a superior quality, being, from its thinness, tenacity, brightness and softness, fit for a variety of economic purposes. It is in appearance and strength similar to English flax, though the fibres are somewhat thinner. In Madras, where it also grows wild, it is selected by the natives as the strongest material for bow-strings, gins, and tiger-traps ; but in Bengal it is never manufactured for trade. In Bombay it is known as a fibre-yielding plant, but does not appear to be cultivated to any extent."*

26. It is evident, therefore, that by fostering the

Double benefit to be derived from the cultivation of such fibres. cultivation of this plant, and others like it, Government would be conferring a double

* Report of the cultivation of, and trade in, Jute in Bengal, and on Indian Fibres available for the manufacture of Paper. By Baboo Hem Chunder Ker, Deputy Magistrate, on special duty to enquire into the production of, and trade in, Jute. (Page 4.)

benefit,—it would increase its revenue, and at the same time provide a remedy against absolute starvation in case of bad harvests; while on the principle that industry begets industry, some new source of wealth might arise or be resuscitated, just as the opening of the jute trade caused the revival of the whale fishery in Baffin's Bay.

27. As a general rule, I am no advocate for Government interfering with, or trying to improve, the culture of the crops already established; for past experience has shewn that an absence of practical knowledge has invariably led to failure, while, at the same time, the increased expense attending Government or European agency absorbs any profit that may accrue from an improved system of culture. The following extract from a Government Blue Book, published in 1874, supports these views:—
" Owing to ignorance of the country and its agricultural customs, the farms established by Government have not made an average out-turn equal to that obtained by the native cultivators. These farms have been started with the intention of teaching agriculture to the natives of India; the real lesson has been, that, given their means and soil and climate, it is absolutely necessary first to master their system. In fact, the native cultivators know a great deal more than they were given credit for."* Again,

marginal note: Government interference with *established* crops not desirable.

* Statement, exhibiting the Moral and Material Progress and Condition of India during the year 1872-73. Ordered by the House of Commons to be printed 2nd June, 1874.

neither Government nor European enterprise can compete with indigenous labor in the cultivation of the established crops, because in the case of the former all profits are absorbed by a highly-paid supervising establishment, which, though not requisite in England, is essential in India; while the latter only cultivate areas which their families can work, or exchange labor for labor, thus reducing the expenditure to a minimum.

28. When a new plant is to be introduced, however, the case is different; and if the cultivation of the *Calotropis* is to be accomplished, Government must take the initiative by granting pecuniary aid, only closely observing the principle laid down by Sir George Campbell, "not to farm directly ourselves, but to select intelligent experts to farm after their own fashion on our land."

In the case of a new plant, on the other hand, Government may most fitly take the initiative.

29. The advance system is already known in India as *takkávi*, and dates almost from our first occupation of the country. It was instituted to provide for agricultural improvements, which, without these advances, the people are not in a position to undertake. From the Government Blue Book, so often referred to, we learn that a "consolidation of the laws on the subject of *takkávi* was necessary; and in the end of September, 1871, the Land Improvement Act (which is an Act to consolidate and amend the Law relating to advances by Government for agricultural improvements) became law. The Act authorizes local

The takkávi, or advance system, in India applicable in this case.

Governments to make rules, prescribing the manner
in which advances may be made, the conditions
under which they may be granted, the arrangements
for securing the due expenditure of advances, and
for the proper inspection and maintenance of works
constructed by their means. Any landlord or
tenant desiring to make improvements of land in
which he is in possession or occupation, may make
an application to the collector for an advance, stating
the nature and amount of security for repayment,
which is recoverable by the same means as arrears
of revenue. But an advance to a tenant is not to
be made if the landlord dissents." It is to this
system we owe the introduction of opium, indigo,
silk, and other products, and it is to this system we
must look, for some time to come, for assistance in
the introduction of all new agricultural commodities.*

30. To shew that the *takkávi* system is not, so
far as its principle is concerned, confined
to the East, I would cite one or two
instances in which advances have been made nearer
home. When the growth of flax was a desideratum,
a grant of £1,000 a year was made to the Royal
Flax Improvement Society for the culture of flax in
Ireland, a measure which, though unnecessary in
England, has certainly been most useful in that

The system *(tak-kávi)* is not con-fined to the East.

* Referring to the early history of cotton, David Bremner writes :—"A
great impetus was given to the incipient industry by the emperors of the
Yuen dynasty, towards the close of the 13th century. They encouraged,
and in some cases forced, the inhabitants to grow the plant, imposing on
the provinces an annual tribute for cotton wool. In course of time the
people came to see that the crop was a very advantageous one, and they
devoted themselves to its cultivation without further nursing by the
State."—" Great Industries in Great Britain," Part I.

country.   In like manner it will be remembered
that the Russian hemp and flax trade was at one
time dependent on English capital.   Money was
annually sent to different parts of Russia, and agents
were despatched into the country districts to buy up
the quantities which each cultivator had been able to
grow, but could not prepare before the winter, and
the article was not delivered until six months later.
The Earl of Clarendon, in his speech on the Russian
War in the House of Lords, in August, 1855, said :—
" We must consider, too, that the trade with Russia
is usually conducted with English capital; that
English capital has been indispensable in bringing
them to market; that that has entirely ceased, and
that all the industry of the country has, to a great
extent, been paralyzed, while the want of markets
has deprived the Russian proprietor of all that he
had to depend on to meet the expenses to which he
is subject."

31.   In like manner in the case of the *Calotropis*,
The *takkávi* system it may perhaps be necessary for the
as applied to this
subject.   Government in the first instance to provide the funds for the development of this new industry, and as the plant grows on barren waste land
hitherto unutilized no tax need first be levied.   Ultimately a market will have to be found for the new
product through the channel suggested in para. 19;
but I am very sure that so soon as the staple has
been established the merchants will be eager enough
to step in and relieve the Government from all further
responsibility in the matter.

32. Now, as regards the grasses to which I have alluded in the first part of this pamphlet as being suitable for paper manufacture, all that remains here for me to do is to quote from two recognized authorities in corroboration of my views. Referring to *Saccharum munja* (at paragraph 33 of his work, already quoted), Dr. Royle writes :—" It is possessed of great tenacity, as is evident from two-inch ropes, of fifty fathoms in length, made from its fibre, being sufficient for dragging their largest (or 1200 maund*) boats up the Indus, and consequently against stream." Baboo Hem Chunder Ker, to whose report I have already referred (at paragraph 35), tells us :—" The leaves of the *Saccharum munja* are twisted into ropes of great strength. The plant grows abundantly in almost every part of Upper India, and has been from a very remote period of antiquity used by the Hindus for making cords. It is a common weed in most parts of Bengal also. Its fibre can be exported at a small cost, and to any extent desirable. *S. sara* is a rank weed like the last. Its leaves are made into ropes, which are very strong and durable, even when exposed to the action of water. Like the *S. munja*, this reed is also considered by Dr. Royle to be suitable for paper-making." The forests in Sind (north of Sewan) are fronted to a depth of half-a-mile to one mile with both these grasses, and it is in this province chiefly that the forests are so overrun with them as to necessitate the

The grasses referred to in Part I., page 33.

---

* A maund is equal, in round numbers, to 80 lbs,

strictest fire conservancy being maintained at a considerable annual expense.

33. With what advantage waste materials, by the aid Waste products as utilized by the chemist. of Chemistry and manufacturing ingenuity, have been converted into great sources of wealth in England, will be gathered from the following quotation from a Lecture by Dr. Lyon Playfair,* and will have the effect, I hope, of teaching us for the future to endeavour to turn to account the many products we have up to the present regarded as rubbish. " Chemistry, like a prudent housewife," Dr. Playfair writes, " economises every scrap. The clippings of the travelling tinker are mixed with the parings of horses' hoofs from the smithy, the cast-off woollen garments of the poorest inhabitants of the sister isle, and soon afterwards, in the form of dyes of brightest blue, grace the dress of courtly dames. The main ingredient of the ink with which I now write was once part of the broken hoop of an old beer-barrel. The bones of dead animals yield the chief constituent of lucifer matches. The dregs of port wine, carefully rejected by the port wine drinker, in decanting his favourite beverage, are taken by him in the morning as seidlitz powders. The offal of the streets, and the washing of coal-gas, re-appear, carefully preserved in the lady's smelling-bottle, or are used by her to flavour blanc-manges for her friends. This economy of art is only in imitation of what we observe in the chemistry of nature. Animals live and die ; their dead bodies passing into putridity, escape

* "Chambers' Journal," Saturday, June 13th, 1874, No. 546.

into the atmosphere, whence plants again mould them into forms of organic life ; and these plants, actually consisting of a past generation of ancestors, form our present food."

34. I would recommend that the promotion of the trade in the five samples of paper manufactured and exhibited by me (referred to in Part I.), should be left entirely in the hands of the Forest Department in whose immediate district the fibres from which they were made exist. The mode suggested for introducing other fibres into the market should, however, be observed in this instance, as in all others appertaining to fibres. In this connection, I would beg leave to suggest that the development of this subject might with great advantage to the Government be placed in the hands of a small body of men who would take a real interest in the concern. Several such men are to be found in the Forest Department, although it does not of course follow that because a man belongs to that Department he has a taste or aptitude for such work as I have referred to. Indeed, I have myself heard a brother officer, who prided himself on his knowledge and love of pure forestry, ridicule the idea of being expected to turn his attention to the culture of lac, silk, rheea fibres, and others, which form no part of his legitimate duties ; while others, again, delight in such work, and are only too glad of an opportunity of doing anything to advance such undertakings. These latter are the men whose co-operation Government will probably desire to

obtain; and if I might be allowed to offer a suggestion, I would strongly urge upon Her Majesty's Secretary of State for India, and the Indian Government, the advisability of selecting from their Forest Department a few officers who have shewn a special fitness for the development of other natural forest products than timber, and forming them into a corps under the direction of a duly qualified officer, known to have a special taste in this direction. The details of such a scheme would, of course, have to be elaborated with care, and if the Government wished it, I would very gladly draw up for approval a plan, by which the work could be done with little or no increase of present expenditure. Having given the matter much earnest attention, it would be a pleasure to me to be of any service in enabling the Government to come to a conclusion as to the advisability of taking steps in the matter. I have already drafted a scheme which might, I venture to think, be carried out with advantage to the Government, and I shall gladly submit it for the consideration of the authorities should I be permitted to do so. In my humble opinion, the development of the fibre trade of India is a matter of sufficient importance to justify the creation of a new branch of the Department of Agriculture, Revenue and Commerce; and that there is ample work to occupy the attention of such a Department will not, I think, be denied. Probably the Government would feel that it would be more satisfactory to detach, if possible, a small body of men from the Forest Depart-

E

ment for this special work, than to add it to the already heavy duties of all the number of that or any other Department; for each branch of the Service has at present its time fully engaged. The experiment would in any case be very interesting, and it might in the first instance be made on a small scale, by planting, say 2,000 acres in Berar, or the Central Provinces, where the *Calotropis* is known to grow wild over a scattered expanse of country, and where there is no lack of sterile land, which, though peculiarly suited to the *Calotropis*, is absolutely unfitted for the growth of any other crop. If at the the same time another little experiment were made in the Punjab or Sind (which is *par excellence* the land of the *Calotropis*), the Government would very soon find whether there was any probability of the scheme coming to anything. Every effort should, of course, be made to reduce the cost of production (by concentrating labour, and by encouraging the cultivation of the plant in uniform blocks, thereby facilitating transport) and of the manufacture of the fibre.* It may be said, with reference to my suggestion that a body of men should be taken from the Forest Department to carry out the scheme I advocate, that this Department cannot afford men. This is, of course, a point for the consideration of Government and the heads of the Department; but

---

* I would here remind the authorities that before proceeding to outdoor experiments it would be necessary to provide a machine for the extraction of the fibre. This done, the experiments could be extended to the plant in its wild state; and finally artificial cultivation could be resorted to if trials warranted it. I would here invite the reader's attention to the Appendix.

I would not have it supposed that my project could not be carried out by any other machinery. I merely suggest what I consider best; but so confident am I that the Government will find it to its advantage to give the scheme a trial, that I would recommend the appointment of a few native overseers, with one con-trolling officer (European), rather than that the matter should be allowed to drop. The only points which I consider absolutely essential to the fair conduct of even a preliminary experiment are two. In the first place, the men engaged, whether Europeans or natives, should devote themselves entirely to this work; and in the second place, a European Superintendent-in-Chief is a *sine quâ non*.

35. The question of transport is one of consider-
Cost of transport requires careful consideration. able importance in connection with the expense of any undertaking. This is sometimes so heavy as to necessitate the abandonment of what might otherwise have proved a profitable business. The stalks of the American maize, which, for years past, has been known to be better material for paper than straw, was for a long time rendered value-less purely on account of the cost of exporting it; but recently we hear of the material being brought over at a cheap rate as ballast, and utilized for paper by C. Townsend Hook and Co., of Snodland, Kent.

36. Should Her Majesty's Secretary of State for
The superintending officer should visit officially the chief British manufactories. India and the Indian Government decide upon adopting my views, I would beg leave to offer one more suggestion, which is, that the officer selected for the development of the project

should be directed to visit some of the principal rope, paper, and textile manufacturers in England, Scotland, and Ireland, with a view to getting an insight into the technical and practical treatment in their raw state of the materials to which his future attention will have to be turned. By knowing the requirements of the trade, we are most likely to provide for them with the least chance of failure, while much unnecessary correspondence would be avoided, and time and money saved. My recent visit to Mr. Towgood's paper mill, near Cambridge, forcibly reminded me of the maxim of Tregold, the great engineer, that " *one ounce of practice outweighed a ton of theory.*" No reading could have supplied me with the vast amount of information I gained during the few hours spent in inspecting the manufacture of paper, from the sorting of the rags to the final stage of its preparation.*

37. In conclusion, I think it well to give in a **Jute and Calotropis gigantea contrasted in detail** form, which will readily catch the eye, a comparison between jute and the Calotropis, the plant, the cultivation of which I specially advocate. I accordingly contrast them in parallel columns. The information regarding jute is extracted from the Report by Baboo Hem Chunder Kerr, who was specially deputed to enquire into the cultivation of jute, and from Dr. Forbes Watson's Report on Rheea.

* I take this opportunity of recording my deep sense of gratitude to Mr. Towgood, the owner of the Sawston Paper Mills, Cambridge, and his polite manager, for the painstaking manner in which they practically illustrated to me the art of paper-making from beginning to end.

The page references in the left-hand column are to the Jute Commission and Dr. Watson's Report, and those in the right-hand column are to the paragraphs in this pamphlet.

Jute.

LOCALITY.

Opinions vary; but on the whole, the balance of evidence is decidedly in favour of high or súna lands as the best for jute, provided all other conditions necessary for its healthy growth be attainable. Low lands and "churs," however, are not unsuited to the growth of the plant, "churs" ranking midway between the two. (P. 23, 24.)

CLASS OF SOIL.

Some are in favour of "rich clay and sand in equal or nearly equal proportions"; others prefer "soil consisting of a mixture of clay and sand, or sand combined with alluvial deposits"; while others again, grow it "on land which is neither inundated nor dry, the soil being loam, i.e. half clay and half sand." (P. 25.)

Calotropis Gigantea.

LOCALITY.

Wild or arid wastes, unsuited to the growth of any other plant. Land that has hitherto yielded no revenue. The plant will also thrive on land suited to the growth of jute, and accommodates itself to most tropical soils and climate. (Part II., pars. 3—35.)

CLASS OF SOIL.

Immaterial. Anything will do, from sand to a rich loam. (Part II., pars. 3—35.)

Climatic Conditions.

" Too much rain at the beginning of the season and early floods are equally destructive to the young plants, and injurious to the prospects of the crop. Alternate rain and sunshine are found to be the most congenial to the jute plant, but excessive rain after the plant has attained a height of 2 or 3 feet will not prove materially injurious so long as no water lodges at the roots."
. . " My inquiries lead me to believe that it suffers less injury from excess of rainfall than from entire want of it. It is admitted on all hands that drought always stunts their growth, and very often, as we ourselves observed during the present year in Rungpore, and Goalparah even, destroys them if not sufficiently developed." (P. 26.)

Climatic Conditions.

Thrives in the most arid parts of the province of Sind as well as in the humid province of Burma. (Part II., par. 25.)

Mode of Sowing.

" The seeds are sown broadcast on a clear sunny day, and covered over with a thin crust of earth, either by the hand or by a *hindá*, or harrow, or a *moï*, or ladder, or, as in Bhaugulpore and Julpigoree, by beams of wood drawn over the field by oxen." (P. 29.)

Mode of Sowing.

Broadcast, without any prior preparation or subsequent labour. (Part I., par. 30.)

Weeding.

" Once or twice between sowing and reaping." (P. 30.)

Weeding.

None.

Mode of Manufacturing Fibre.

"After reaping, the stalks are tied into bundles, and by some immediately submerged, but by others allowed to dry in the sun for a few days before subjecting the bundles to the retting process, which occupies on an average about eight days, the period being regulated according to circumstances. In steeping the stalks in water, they are covered with a layer of refuse tops of the jute-plants, or other jungle plants or with clods of earth, sometimes with cow-dung, sometimes with trunks of plantain trees, or logs of the date-tree, and sometimes with straw smeared with mud. . . . While the bundles are under water they are examined from time to time to test how far the rotting has progressed. When complete, the process of separation most generally followed is to beat or shake the stalks in the water in which it is steeped till the glutinous substance in the bark is entirely washed away. The fibres at first detached partially from the pulp, but by continued agitation in the water gradually disintegrate from it altogether. Next follows the washing of the fibre, and ultimate drying on lines." (P. 31—33.)

MANURE.

The land is sometimes manured with cow-dung, but when the soil is poor oil-cake is substituted. Sheep's dung and urine have also been successfully tried. (P. 28.)

Mode of Manufacturing Fibre.

After reaping, the stalks are tied up in bundles and carried home. The stems are then placed in the sun to dry for two days, when they are macerated (by being beaten on a block of wood with a mallet) until the cuticle or outer bark separates freely from the epidirmis or true bark, and the latter comes away readily from the ligneous part. After half-a-dozen lashes or so, the fibre is produced in a fit state for the market.

MANURE.

None at all necessary.

The Out-turn of Clean, Marketable Fibre.

According to Dr. Forbes Watson, 12—1500 is given as the yield per acre, but this must be the maximum out-turn of the most prolific jute-growing district(Backerjunge). According to the Report of the Jute Commission, the out-turn per acre in 1872, the above figures are given as the largest yield, and 160 lbs. per acre as the minimum. Baboo Hem Chunder Kerr, alluding to his comparative statement, writes: "The above table gives an average of 5 maunds 14 seers per beegah (or 850 lbs. per acre) all round. This is, however, not a true index of the actual produce, the average being affected by the scanty produce of a large number of unfavourable districts. Taking the large jute-growing districts alone, the average would be about 6 maunds per beegah (or about 960 lbs. per acre.) (P. 36.)

The Out-turn of Clean, Marketable Fibre.

Under the present rude and wasteful system of preparing the fibre (which shows a waste of 25 per cent.) one acre is said to yield 582 lbs., or 727 lbs. where waste is guarded against. (Part I., par. 30.)

Cost of Cultivation.

"This fluctuates from Rs. 1-15 to Rs. 17 (or 1s. 10d. to £1 13s. 2d.) per acre per annum. Bearing in mind that almost universally the cultivation, except in the case of a limited number of the more wealthy class of ryots, is carried on by the ryots themselves and their families, and hired labour, hired ploughs and cattle are very rarely called into use, it must be evident that the exact out-of-pocket expense is no criterion of the actual cost. These figures, therefore, as also those showing the cost of pre-

Cost of Cultivation.

£2 9s. 8d. per acre, and when once this has been incurred no further outlay is requisite each year as with jute. The Collector of Shikarpore seems to consider that cultivation is unnecessary, and that there is sufficient of the plant growing wild in his collectorate alone to keep twenty factories employed. (Part II., par. 30.)

paring the fibre, must be accepted with reservation, as they represent rather what would be the case if hired labour were employed than the cost actually incurred." (P. 37.)

MARKET VALUE.

From £18 to £21. (G. and J. A. Noble's Monthly Circular, Nov. 9th, 1877.)

IS THE CULTIVATION OF JUTE REMUNERATIVE?

It is generally maintained that jute would not be remunerative in its cultivation, if the labour employed in its cultivation and preparation were to be paid for. The most out-of-pocket item is rent of land. (P. 37.)

IS JUTE AN EXHAUSTIVE CROP?

The Collector of Rungpore reports that "jute is never grown for two years running on the same land, and in *pergunnahs* Bahirbund and Bhiturbund it is grown every second or third year by rotation." Baboo Hem Chunder Kerr writes: "After a careful and mature consideration of the local Reports, and the evidence of the large body of agriculturalists and experienced persons whom the Commis-

MARKET VALUE.

According to the opinion of experts, from £30 to £40 per ton. (Part I., par. 32.)

IS THE CULTIVATION OF THE CALOTROPIS REMUNERATIVE?

This question can decidedly be answered in the affirmative, after careful perusal of the foregoing facts. The plant grows wild in arid wastes, and is valueless for any other crop. It is independent of drought and blight, and the land on which it grows wild, and may be multiplied, is not subject to taxation. The only impediment to its introduction into trade is the absence of mechanical force in the preparation of the fibre, and this obstacle is easily to be conquered, if we go the right way to work. (*Passim.*)

IS CALOTROPIS AN EXHAUSTIVE CROP?

Decidedly not. After being cut down it reproduces itself within twelve months, when it is ready for another cutting, having attained its original dimensions. And so on (Part I., par. 30.)

sion have personally consulted in the several jute-growing districts, I have no hesitation in saying that jute does more : generally speaking it exhausts and impoverishes the soil to a much greater extent than other crops." (P. 40 and 41.)

WHAT IS THE RESISTING POWER OF JUTE TO THE ACTION OF HIGH-PRESSURE STEAM ?

"Loss per cent, after exposure for 2 hours in steam, at 15 lbs. extra pressure, followed by boiling in water (212 degrees F.) for 3 hours, 19.20."

"Loss per cent. after further exposure for 4 hours to steam and water at 15 lbs. extra pressure, 2.19. (Dr. Watson's Report on Rhea, p. 5.)

WHAT IS THE MEAN DIAMETER (MICROMETRIC) OF JUTE ?

Diameter of Fibres.							
Ordinary.				Ultimate.			
		Mean.				Mean.	
Min. Decimals.	Max. Decimals.	Decimals.	Vul. Fractions.	Min. Decimals.	Max. Decimals.	Decimals.	Vul. Fractions.
.00142	.00374	.00258	1/380	.000420	.000647	.000533	1/1900

(Dr. Watson's Report on Rhea, p. 6.)

WHAT IS THE RESISTING POWER OF THE CALOTROPIS TO THE ACTION OF HIGH-PRESSURE STEAM ?

Loss per cent., after exposure for 2 hours in steam at 15 lbs. extra pressure, followed by boiling in water (212 degrees F.) for 3 hours, 3.19.

Loss per cent. after further exposure for 4 hours to steam and water at 15 lbs. extra pressure, 2.28. (Dr. Watson's Report on Rhea, p. 5.)

WHAT IS THE MEAN DIAMETER (MICROMETRIC) OF THE CALOTROPIS ?

Diameter of Fibres.							
Ordinary.				Ultimate.			
		Mean.				Mean.	
Min. Decimals.	Max. Decimals.	Decimals.	Vul. Fractions.	Min. Decimals.	Max. Decimals.	Decimals.	Vul. Fractions.
.00250	.00530	.00390	1/260	.000325	.000663	.000494	1/2000

Dr. Watson's Report on Rhea, p. 6.)

How is Jute Classed by Dr. Forbes Watson?	How is the Calotropis Classed by Dr. Forbes Watson?
As a second-class fibre. (Report on Rheea, p. 6.)	As a first-class fibre. (Report on Rheea, p. 6.)

I append a list of fibre-yielding plants, to which I desire most respectfully to draw the attention of the Indian Government. Most of them are indigenous to the country, and those that are not have become so naturalised as to accommodate themselves to most latitudes. They require no high or expensive culture; their fibres may be extracted by the most simple and inexpensive process; and the last two named will grow in poor, stony, dry situations, or sandy, salt soils.

1.—Grewia Asiatica.
2.—Pandanus Odoratissimus.
3.—Daphne.
4.—Agave Americana.
5.—Sanseviera Zeylonica.

APPENDIX.

I had completed the draft of my pamphlet when the following correspondence reached me. 1 print it here, not only because it refers to the five samples of paper spoken of at page 8, but because it confirms what I have said as to the Conservators of Forests being unable to undertake more work than is already allotted to them. The Additional Conservator justly says :—"*As the Forest Department is at present constituted, and with the work in hand of selecting reserves, &c., it has not the time to enter into experiments with regard to the disposal of minor forest products.*" These views, emanating from Mr. Ribbentrop, carry extra weight, for this gentleman's great administrative ability, zeal, and energy have gained for him the distinguished and exceptional office of Additional Conservator of Forests.

I do not think, however, our fibre-yielding Indian plants can fairly be called "*minor forest products.*" If the fibres which I have mentioned ultimately prove marketable commodities, they may, perhaps, form one of the principal sources of revenue to all our forests, other than those where teak, sál, and sandalwood are grown.

The reasons given by Mr. Ribbentrop in support of his opinion that the cost of producing the fibre will exceed its value when produced, do not convince me. Granted that, as compared with other trees, the Ficus are at present scattered over a considerable area, there is no valid reason why they should not be brought within a convenient distance of the factory, if their fibre is of sufficient value to warrant such steps being taken. And so likewise with *Broussonetia papyrifera* and *Streblus aspera.* But until the true value of these fibres has been *finally* determined, no advantageous action on an extensive scale can be taken in the matter.

When Mr. Ribbentrop speaks of Rs. 35 per ton as the cost of freight, he means, I presume, the freight on a single ton or two, and does not intend to imply that the average cost per ton on a large consignment, sent by a chartered vessel, would be so heavy as that. And to judge the prospects of the trade fairly, it must be assumed, unless the assumption be proved untenable, that large quantities will be dealt with. Moreover, there is no reason why this item of expenditure should not be reduced to a minimum by shipping the fibre as ballast. I have already treated this matter in full detail *(vide* pp. 67, *ante),* so that no more need be said on the subject here.

I am much gratified at the compliment paid me by the Chief Commissioner of British Burma, in ruling that my proposal remain in abeyance until I return to Burma; but I should have preferred had my suggestion been carried out, and a sample consignment been sent to me while I was in England. I should then, I respectfully submit, have been in a much better position to develop the scheme, and further the interests of Government, than I can possibly be in India. I have learnt by experience that work of this kind can be more satisfactorily accomplished by means of personal interview than by correspondence, or by employing third parties. For example, it is not every dealer in paper, textile fabrics and rope, who is sufficiently acquainted with our Eastern fibres to allow of his corresponding on the subject; but if such a man can have samples placed before him, and definite and exhaustive information supplied on the spot, my experience has been that he is very glad to avail himself of any new source of wealth. And, with the utmost deference to the opinions of others, I think it will

be ultimately found that, as far as the matter I am advocating is concerned, this is the only method of procedure
which will lead to success.

As regards the 15 tons of *Calotropis* fibre, which I recommended should be sent to England for experiment (*vide*
p. 50), it appears from a Memorandum by the Collector of Shikarpore—which reached me through Col. Sir W. Merewether
—that although the *Calotropis* grows wild in prolific
abundance throughout Sind, the cost of producing the fibre
far exceeds its market value. With a view, then, to reduce
the cost of the preparation of the fibre (by substituting machinery for manual labour), I applied at once for one cwt. of
the dried stems of the plant to experiment upon, undertaking
to meet all costs if the Acting Commissioner did not feel warranted in supplying me at Government expense. This application, however, was rejected by the Acting Commissioner, Mr.
Melvill, and I was directed to apply to the Bombay Government or the Government of India for what I required. The
balance of my leave in England is too short for me to adopt
this course; it must therefore remain with the authorities
here to decide upon the action to be taken.

Inasmuch as the same opinion prevails in some quarters
regarding the relative merits of the fibre obtained from the
green and from the dry stems of the *Calotropis*, which once
existed with respect to the comparative merit of fibre
obtained from the green and dried stems of the rheea, I was
induced to apply to the Commissioner for one cwt. of the
dried stems of the former for experiment with certain
different machines I know of, for I see no reason why the
general opinion may not prove as incorrect in this instance
as it was in the case of rheea. Dr. Forbes Watson, in his
Report on Rheea, to which I have had already constantly to
refer, writes :—" With regard to the last point, referring to
the best mode of preparing the fibre, there is evidence that
the process of separating the fibre need not be restricted to

the green stems, and that retting, if carried out under conditions not unlike those in the usual flax and hemp retting, may possibly be employed with advantage " (p. 4).

The offer of prizes for a machine adapted for the treatment of fresh stems of rheea, as cut from the plant, is in no way inconsistent with Dr. Watson's statement, because, on grounds of economy, it has been found expedient to prepare the fibre in India. "Except during the hot, dry weather preceding the rains in Upper India (where rheea grows best), it is very difficult so to dry the stems that no fermentation or mildew shall occur."* The case of the *Calotropis*, however, is quite different. The climate of the province where it grows in greatest abundance is dry—the maximum rain-fall not exceeding 15 to 30 inches, while the plant attains maturity in the hot season. The disadvantages of importing dried rheea stems are therefore not applicable to the *Calotropis;* but the advantages attending the use of the dried stems of the rheea, as enumerated by Dr. Watson, are decidedly applicable to the *Calotropis.* The author writes :—
" The advantages of using dried stems may be briefly enumerated as follows :—The greater facility in designing machinery, and the probable simplicity of its working, when compared with that intended to work the green stems. As a matter of course, it is easier to break up and to remove the wooden core of the stem, if the latter is perfectly dry and broken, than if it is moist and flexible. Then, as regards the important point of removing the outer brown cuticle of the bark, if the dry stems are operated upon, this cuticle is very friable, and easily reduced to dust and shaken out; whilst in the green it requires a scraping action to remove it—an action of all the most difficult to obtain by mechanical means."

* Notification issued by the Government of India, Department of Revenue, Agriculture, and Commerce, dated Simla, 31st August, 1877, No. 45.

Further on Dr. Watson tells us, in the same Report, that "the fibre obtained from the dried stems (of the rheea) amounts to about 20 to 28 per cent. of the weight of the dried stems, which corresponds to about 4 to 6 per cent. in the weight of fresh stems."—There is no reason, physical or other, that I know of, why the dried stems of the *Calotropis* should not give similar favourable results. However this may be, I would very earnestly urge the expediency of giving this plant a fair trial. If the experiment fails, the next point to which attention should be turned is the introduction of a machine capable of working the raw material. We should then be precisely at the stage at which the Rheea project rests at present.

The following is the Correspondence referred to above :—

From the Additional Conservator of Forests, British Burma.
To the Secretary to the Chief Commissioner, British Burma.

No. 645.
___
141.

Dated Rangoon, 5th July, 1875.

Sir,—I have the honour to forward copy of Mr. Strettell's letter, dated 2nd May, 1877, to my address, regarding papers to be made from—

> *Broussonetia papyrifera.*
> *Streblus aspera.*
> *Ficus infectoria.*
> *Ficus Rumphii.*
> *Ficus excelsa.*

I would respectfully state that the Forest Department, as at present constituted, and with the work in hand of selecting reserves, &c., has not the time to enter into experiments with regard to the disposal of minor forest produce. Moreover, although the trees enumerated are plentiful, they

F

are scattered about the forests, and the collection, the transport to Rangoon, the manufacture, &c., and ultimately the freight of at least Rs. 35 per ton, would, in my opinion, amount to more than the value of the stock.

I have, &c., &c.,

(Signed) B. Ribbentrop,

Additional Commissioner of Forests,

B.B.

Forest Department, No. 331.

123.

From G. C. Kynoch, Esq., *Assistant to the Secretary to the Chief Commissioner, B.B.*

To the Additional Conservator of Forests, B.B.

Dated Rangoon, 6th August.

Sir,—I am directed to acknowledge the receipt of your letter No. 645—141, dated 4th ult., forwarding copy of a correspondence received from Mr. G. W. Strettell, Deputy Conservator of Forests, now in England, regarding the manufacture of paper from the bark of certain trees.

2. In reply, I am to request that you will communicate a copy of your letter under acknowledgment to Mr. Strettell, and suggest that the consideration of this proposal should remain in abeyance until he returns to Burma.

I have, &c.,

(Signed) G. C. Kynoch,

Assistant to the Secretary C.C.

No. 4,099 of 1877,

Revenue Department.

From F. D. Melvill, Esq., *Acting Commissioner in Sind.*

Dated Kurrachee, 15th October, 1877.

Sir,—In reply to your letter dated 11th September, in

which you allude to previous correspondence with my predecessor, on the subject of *Uk* and *Sur* fibres, and ask that one cwt. of dried stalks of *Uk* should be sent to you, and, secondly, that a similar quantity of the *Sur* fibre should be despatched to you, with accurate calculations of the cost incurred, I have the honour to reply, as follows :—

2. Some *Uk* fibre was apparently sent to you in May, 1876.* The previous correspondence to which you allude was not left on record by Sir William Merewether. But whilst I concur entirely with you in the advantage of developing the resources of India, I am of opinion that isolated and spasmodic attempts to develop a new industry are unsatisfactory. I would therefore recommend your addressing the Government of Bombay, or the Government of India, in the Agricultural Department, on the subject, who, if they consider that the experiment will be beneficial, and has not already been tried, will doubtless render you every assistance in the matter. I think this course will, in the end, offer you the largest prospect of success.

I have, &c.,

(*Signed*)   F. D. MELVILL,

Acting Commissioner in Sind.

From the Acting Commissioner in Sind.

Sir,—In reply to your letter of the 1st ult., I have the honour to refer you to my letter, No. 4,099, of the 15th *idem.* If you would address Government on the subject of procuring the *Uk* stalks, and the *Sur* fibre, your proposal will, I am sure, receive the consideration it deserves.

I have, &c.,

(*Signed*)   F. D. MELVILL,

Acting Commissioner in Sind.

---

* Quite correct. This sample formed the embryo of my scheme, which was set in motion in February, 1877. It was the DRIED STEMS of the plant I now applied for, and not the prepared fibre.   G. W. S.

Woodlands, Keymer,
Dated 14th November, 1877.

To F. D. MELVILL, Esq., *Acting Commissioner in Sind.*

Sir,—I have the honour to acknowledge, with many thanks, the receipt of yours, No. 4,099, dated 15th ult., in the Revenue Department, wherein you express disapproval of the course I have pursued for the introduction into the home market of certain fibres indigenous to Sind, and suggest what appears to you the correct procedure to be observed.

2. In reply, I beg respectfully to state that the steps I have hitherto taken for the development of the new source of revenue under notice, have—so to speak—been at the request of your predecessor, and in accordance with the wishes expressed by him. In applying, therefore, direct to your administration for a sample consignment of dried *Uk* stalks and *Sur* fibre, you will perceive I was authorized to do so. My second letter, offering to pay for the sample of dried *Uk* stalks, will have indicated the uncertainty I felt as to the light in which you might accept my requisition, and as matters have turned out it is fortunate I took the precautionary step, for I am quite satisfied of the importance and feasibility of the industry I desire to float for the benefit of Government, and am prepared, at all hazards, to carry through my project, though the cost of founding the trade devolves on me—provided, of course, I receive the hearty co-operation of the authorities, and which I have every reason to hope will not be withheld.

The sample consignment of *Uk* alluded to in the 2nd paragraph of your letter under reply—but which only came to hand last January—may be regarded as the embryo of the business I hope ultimately to create. By means of that sample, I was able to ascertain the true commercial value of the fibre, and I have the authority of the principal manufacturers of rope, paper and textile fabrics for stating that the staple is superior to most of the first-class fibres known to the home market, and that it will find a ready sale provided it can be imported in sufficient quantities, and at a reasonable price. The first proviso may be accepted as granted, but the second remains to be proved. According to the estimate supplied me by your predecessor (Sir William Merewether) one hundred pounds sterling per ton is the lowest figure at which the fibre could be landed in *London ;* a price that at once closes the door to competition. I am, however, in hopes that, by substituting machinery for hand labor, we will be able sufficiently to reduce the estimate as to admit of the fibre being brought on the market at a saleable price.

I am aware that a similar idea exists regarding the unfitness of the dried stems of the *Uk* for conversion into fibre, as once prevailed in respect to *Rheea,* but, in the same manner as the latter opinion has proved a popular fallacy, I have reason to believe that the theory respecting *Uk* will be found false. However this may be, it is but right that a fair trial should be made, and then, if the experiment fails, we must next turn our attention to devise a machine that will work the raw material ; but, to say a plant that yields a first-class fibre, that grows wild in prolific abundance in most parts of India, that thrives best on lands absolutely unfitted for any other profitable culture, and that is not influenced by drought, cannot be imported at a saleable price, appears to me too unreasonable, and I have therefore set myself the task of solving the problem.

Under the foregoing circumstances, therefore, I trust you will favour me with the sample of dried *Uk* stems already applied for, *plus* the same quantity of *Sur* fibre, the charges on which I shall be prepared to meet. I would, however, earnestly beg that a detailed memo. of costs incurred may accompany the letter advising the despatch of the consignment.

As the season for collecting *Uk* (for fibre) will expire towards the latter end of December, I respectfully trust you will see fit to order the collection and shipment of my requisition at as early a date as practicable. With every apology for this intrusion on your time,

I have, &c.,
G. W. S.

Woodlands, Keymer,
Hassock's Gate, Sussex.
Dated 11th September, 1877.

To the Commissioner in Sind.

Sir,—In reference to a lengthy correspondence I have had with Col. Sir William Merewether, regarding the introduction of the *Uk* and *Sur* fibres into England, it appears to me that the only impediment to the successful development of a trade in the former is the heavy expense attending the preparation of the fibre, which has been estimated by the Collector of Shikarpore at about £60 to £70 per ton. This charge appears to me very high, in comparison with the manufacture of jute and *Sur*, both of which—I should fancy—entail a more elaborate process of manipulation, and land rent is levied on the land it grows. However, there is no doubt a good reason for the disparity unknown to me.

2. I would venture to suggest that the barrier to the utilization of *Uk* is to be overcome by substituting machine power for the manual extraction of the fibre, which would reduce the cost of fabrication to a reasonable figure —say £7 per ton. I would respectfully recommend to your consideration the introduction of such a machine into Sind. In the event, however, of this proposal not meeting with your approval, perhaps you will not object to send me (to the care of Messrs. Grindlay and Co., 55, Parliament Street,) one cwt. of the dried stems of the *Uk*, when I will see whether the fibre cannot be extracted in England at a remunerative figure. Care must be taken to thoroughly dry the stems to guard against fermentation *en route;*—and further, I respectfully solicit the exact cost of such consignment—in detail—may be supplied me.

3. The value of the fibre for textile fabrics, paper, and rope, is universally acknowledged by manufacturers of the respective trades; while the enormous demand for new material for these industries is sufficient inducement, I hope, to stimulate our efforts to introduce them into European markets. As the originator of this project, I am most anxious that it should not fall through, and you may rest assured I will devote my best and careful attention to carry the business out to a successful end.

4. Now, in reference to this *Sur* fibre :—According to the data supply by Col. Sir William Merewether, it appears that the *bonâ fide* fibre can be purchased at Sukkur at £3 10s. per ton ; to this, if £1 10s. be added for contingent expenses, including freight, £5 per ton would represent the cost at which this fibre might be landed in England.

5. This grass, as you are doubtless aware, abounds in Sind, and as it is irrepressible (reproducing itself within twelve months after the first cutting) an unlimited and constant supply can be guaranteed; while the substitution

of machinery for manual labour would reduce the cost 50 per cent. at least.

I am not in a position at present to speak positively as to the price this fibre will realize here, but judging of its worth by the prices valuable paper-producing materials fetch in England, I am of opinion £5 per ton will leave ample room for the home merchants to embark in the speculation; so that, for the present, I do not think mechanical aid need be resorted to, although I should remind you that the same machine that will work *Uk* will be equally well suited to the grasses.

If you will kindly sanction 1 cwt. of this fibre being sent me, at the same time as the *Uk*, I will be able to ascertain its commercial value, and report to you accordingly. It will be necessary—in this instance as that of the *Uk*—that I am informed of the actual cost of the consignment, to enable me to supply the required information to merchants here; who will never give an order unless they are satisfied of the price at which the material is to be had in London, plus other information which I can furnish.

As my stay in England is rapidly drawing to a close, I will perhaps be pardoned asking to be informed, by return post, your decision in the matter.

I am, &c.,

(Signed)   G. W. STRETTELL.

To the Commissioner of Sind.

Sir,—In my letter of the 11th ult., I solicited the favour of your kindly sanctioning a consignment of 1 cwt. of *Uk*, and the same quantity of *Sur* being sent me, at the expense of Government.

In the event of your not feeling disposed to comply with my application, I beg respectfully to state that I shall be happy to pay all expenses attending the shipment of 1 cwt. of dried *Uk* stalks, with which I desire to make experiments for the ultimate benefit of Government.

To save time, I beg the consignment may be forwarded by a canal steamer.

I have, &c.,
(Signed)   G. W. STRETTELL.

No. 5,161 of 1877.

Revenue Department.

From J. D. MELVILL, Esq., *Acting Commissioner in Sind.*

To G. W. STRETTELL, Esq., *Deputy Conservator of Forests, Woodlands, Keymer, Hassock's Gate, Sussex.*

Commissioners' Office, Camp Garki Kathanda,
20th December, 1877.

Sir,—In reply to your letter dated 15th November last, I have the honor to explain that I did not express my disapproval of the course adopted by you, nor is any justification of that course required. But I did clearly, as I hoped, indicate to you the line which I considered it proper for me to adopt in the matter, and I see no reason for departing from it. That line was as follows:—That you should, if you thought fit, apply direct to Government for assistance in this matter, and any orders which they might give would receive my immediate attention. If, however, you do not wish to adopt that course, there are commercial agents in Kurrachee who would doubtless supply what you

G

want. I had neither the funds at my disposal nor the authority of Government to advance such in promoting your endeavours to introduce a new commodity into the English market. Excellent as I believe your proposal to be, it rests with Government, and not with me, to decide what assistance the State should render you in your enterprise.

I have the honour, &c., &c.,

(*Signed*) F. D. MELVILL,

Acting Commissioner in Sind.

BEAL AND CO., PRINTERS BRIGHTON.